Coming
Out
Young
and
Faithful

Coming Out Young and Faithful

Leanne McCall Tigert

and

Timothy J. Brown,

editors

The Pilgrim Press

Cleveland, Ohio

Dedication

WE OFFER THIS BOOK IN MEMORY OF
THE GAY / LESBIAN / BISEXUAL / TRANSGENDER
YOUTH WHO NEVER MADE IT TO ADULTHOOD.
THE ONES WHO TOOK THEIR OWN LIVES
OR HAD THEIR LIVES TAKEN FROM THEM—
BODY OR SOUL.

The Pilgrim Press, Cleveland, Ohio 44115
www.pilgrimpress.com
© Leanne McCall Tigert and Timothy J. Brown

Printed in the United States of America on acid-free paper

Coming out young and faithful / Leanne McCall Tigert and
Timothy J. Brown, editors
     p. cm.
  Includes bibliographical references.
  ISBN 0-8298-1414-0 (pbk.)
   1. Gays—Religious life. 2. Transsexuals—Religious life.
 3. Homosexuality—Religious aspects—Christianity. 4. Gays—
United States—Biography. 5. Church work with gays. 6. Church
work with teenagers. I. Tigert, Leanne McCall, 1957–
II. Brown, Timothy J.

BV4596.G38 C66 2001
261.8'35766—dc21   2001021965

TABLE OF CONTENTS

Preface

Gay, lesbian, bisexual, and transgender youth are speaking and writing about their experience more than ever before. Books and articles are being written, and school and medical conferences focusing on the mental, physical, and social health concerns of these adolescents are taking place across the country. The voices of these youth ring with a truth and passion to which we all need to listen. The information being researched and provided by those who work with g/l/b/t (gay, lesbian, bisexual, and transgender) youth and young adults is invaluable to our efforts in making the world a safer place. Nonetheless, as is often the case in gay, lesbian, bisexual, and transgender issues, there is a gaping void—that is, information about the spiritual and religious concerns and dynamics. In part, this is because most of the work has been done by educators, physicians, and mental health professionals whose fields of focus do not often extend to spirituality. It is also partly due to the secularization of our society. Success is not measured by the depth of one's spiritual self.

For all gay, lesbian, bisexual, and transgender persons, religion can be a particularly painful thorn in our side. For centuries, organized religion has been the biggest culprit of sexual oppression and a regular point of reference for antigay/lesbian/transgender violence. The rhetoric spouted forth in legislative hearings, radio talk shows, and on the street about God's law and what is "natural" and "unnatural" is a weapon of spiritual battering, harming us on all levels of our being.

Gay, lesbian, bisexual, and transgender persons have taken many different paths to cope with the violence of spiritual and religious oppression. Some have remained closely attached to their church/synagogue/temple, working from within to create change. The Welcoming Church movement[1] of many denominations is an example of this powerful internal revitalization when answering the call to liberation and justice-love. Others have walked away and completely detached from any religious organization or custom within which they were raised. I have heard many g/l/b/t adults say that they had no place for religion, if it had no place for them. Others have described religion as a silly waste of time. Still others have been so traumatized by religion that they are completely silenced. Many g/l/b/t persons are creating new forms of liberating spirituality, joining with others to build community and a sense of the sacred in their lives. However people react to and cope with the homophobic injustice that is woven into the very fabric of our culture, recovering from harmful religious messages and connecting with or creating healthy ones is a major step of the journey.

The idea of this book was born in the Youth and Young Adult Ministries Program of the United Church of Christ Coalition of Lesbian, Gay, Bisexual, and Transgender Concerns. When gay, lesbian, bisexual, transgender, and questioning youth and young adults come together in an environment that honors both their sexuality and their spirituality, truths are told and healing happens. With this book, we hope to broaden that experience. Thus we have collected the writings of twenty-one youth and young adults between the ages of fourteen and twenty-four. Intentionally, we have not edited them. They speak for themselves. Some are written by young men and women actively involved and identified with church and/or religious institutions. Others are written by persons with little or no involvement in religious activities who are willing to describe their experiences. Many youth who were contacted and asked to write responded with "I don't care about religion. Why should I waste my time?" Is that because of their age or their coping with oppression? Probably both. Others wrote beautifully, poignantly real submissions. However, because they were too frightened of their parents' response to ask for legal permission, we cannot print them. Still others asked their parents, but were refused. A few have written under pseudonyms. To all of you who wrote or spoke with us, we are deeply grateful. Your words will reach other youth and young adults, and those who care about them. You are making a difference.

This book is organized into three sections. In the beginning, we, as editors, talk about our own experiences of being teenagers and our work with adolescents today. In addition, we use developmental theory and theological dynamics to aid our understanding of the passages g/l/b/t youth and young adults must go through. In the second section, lesbian, gay, bisexual, and transgender youth and young adults speak for themselves. In section three, we have a combination of articles and information for parents, youth workers, and clergy, including liturgical samples and resources for connection with others.

If you are a teenager, we hope this helps you feel less isolated, and that your affirmation of yourself as a spiritual and sexual being, made in the image and likeness of God, takes root and grows. Remember, you are loved. If you are the parent of a gay, lesbian, bisexual, transgender, or questioning adolescent, we hope this brings you hope and relief. Your child is fine. Yet, more than others who do not have to live through sexual oppression that can be so cruel to youth, he/she needs to know your unconditional love and affirmation. You may have some homework to do to keep up with your son or daughter. If you are someone who works with youth, we hope this inspires you to advocate tirelessly for the needs of the g/l/b/t youth and young adults with whom you have contact. They need you to be out as an ally or role model. And they need to know that you are fighting for them. You may never know the difference you make.

The passionate energy of youth embodies the creative energy of God. They are sacred trusts and holy teachers.

There are so many people to whom we are grateful. First and foremost, we thank the youth and young adult writers who agreed to lay open their hearts' journeys. Because they have done this, others will know what it is like to grow into spiritual and emotional health in spite of the forces that seek to condemn. We thank the families and friends who have affirmed them as persons and encouraged them to write. Together, they are all models of hope and reconciliation.

We are grateful to the United Church of Christ Coalition for Lesbian, Gay, Bisexual, and Transgender Concerns, and especially to the Youth and Young Adult Ministries Program. This organization and others like it have become the lifeblood and saving grace for many. We offer a special thanks to Kim Sadler of The Pilgrim Press, whose belief in this work inspired us when we grew weary. Also, we thank Dr. Nan Travers, Rev. Mitzi Eilts, and Rev. Marie Bacchiocchi for their support. Finally, there are many people, some of whom we don't know, who have helped spread the word of this book through youth and young-adult web sites, support groups, and organizations. Thanks to all who have been connected to this project and to the large work of making the world safer for gay, lesbian, bisexual, transgender, and questioning youth and young adults.

Facing a Social Change

LEANNE

As a pastoral counselor I have had the honor to work with many
gay, lesbian, bisexual, transgender, and questioning youth and
young adults. The rawness of their energy and honesty continues
to surprise and invigorate me, while the tenderness of their need
compels me to protect them from harm. Things are different for
g/l/b/t youth and young adults at the beginning of this new mil-
lennium than they were for those of us growing up in the last half
of the 1900s. Yet, things are also the same. Negotiating a path
through the coming out and coming of age process continues to
be both simple and complex. Some kids celebrate their sexuality,
while others struggle fiercely. Most youth know both struggle
and celebration. Some young adults have strong support from
friends and family. Others are harassed physically, sexually, or
verbally. Most have known both. Some of these kids are surrounded by a community of g/l/b/t youth and adults who mirror
healthy, positive images of themselves, while others emerge completely alone, not breathing a word to anyone. Again, most have
a little of both.

Perhaps what has changed the most for youth and young
adults coming out today—as compared to ten, twenty, or thirty
years ago—is the experience of exposure. When I was a
"butch" teen walking down the school hallway, no one jeered

"dyke" or "queer" at me. Just as alternative sexual orientations were not foremost in my consciousness, neither were they in my peers' minds. It was completely taboo to utter the word even if you thought it in the back of your mind. Thus, the silence was deafening and condemning, but the sound was not. Today it is a different story.

Last fall while stacking wood in my backyard, five middle-school boys were standing in the street talking and passing the time. Within a ten-minute conversation, I overheard the word faggot more than sixteen times. I stopped counting at that point. Were they trying to harass me? Perhaps, but I don't believe so. I think they were having a normal conversation, oblivious to the adult next door. Yesterday, I heard about a student who had performed in her high school play. Afterwards, while walking down the hall with her short hair and nose ring, she heard, "Dyke, dyke dyke," chanted at her until she ducked into the restroom, sobbing inside one of the stalls. She is heterosexual. A young, openly gay man who was a leader in forming the diversity support group at his school recently was followed by a carload of teenage males shouting hateful epitaphs and making obscene gestures at him. He locked his doors and drove directly to the police department. The other car pulled away, while one young man mouthed through the window, "We'll get you."

More visibility brings more overt reaction. Almost every study of hate crimes and antigay/lesbian/transgender violence points to an alarming increase of episodes of violence towards those who are g/l/b/t or perceived to be so. In 1993 D'Augelli and Hershberger undertook a study of gay and lesbian youth between the ages of fourteen and twenty-one in fourteen cities across the United States. Eighty percent of those studied reported experiences of verbal abuse, 44 percent felt the threat of attack, 33 percent had objects thrown at them, 30 percent had been chased/followed, 17 percent had been physically assaulted, and 10 percent reported being assaulted with a weapon.[1] Another study of Yale University students reports that 42 percent had been physically abused, and one in five had been assaulted because of their sexual orientation.²

Thus, in order to come out as a gay, lesbian, bisexual, or transgender teen, one has to manage more than just one's sexuality. Each of these adolescents must navigate his or her way through the traumatization of homophobia—living as part of a stigmatized minority.³ As with lesbian, gay, bisexual, and transgender adults, the problem is not the gender identity of one's affectional/sexual attraction. The problem is the meaning that this has been given in society. The difficulty is not that a fifteen-year-old boy has a crush on a boy instead of a girl. The difficulty is that this immediately places him as a member of a dreaded and shamed social group—a group upon which many in our society sanction open season by other males trying to prove their manhood. Lesbian, gay, bisexual, and transgender youth and young adults are perhaps the only social minority that must learn to manage this social identity without active modeling and support from family, friends, or religious community. Thus, more than ever they need us as surrogate family and faithful community.

Teenagers must weave their way through a complex web of social, emotional, cognitive, and spiritual factors to facilitate a healthy self-identity. Coming out and claiming themselves to be part of a hated, humiliated class of persons whose rights are debated daily in newspapers, radio talk shows, and legislative halls across the country can be exhausting. However, to add this to the already demanding list of concerns and developmental tasks of adolescence is often overwhelming.

In recent years, several psychological studies have been undertaken to explore the process by which g/l/b/t youth integrate their sexual identity along with these other developmental factors. In 1989, R. R. Troidan proposed a four-stage model encompassing the child and teenage years. First, he says that children become aware of feeling different from others and begin to experience social isolation. I know that I have sat with countless youth and adults who clearly remember this feeling. In fact, for many it was so significant that it clouds all other memories of childhood. Usually this feeling of difference is related to both sexual orientation and gender identity, such as my own feelings of shame because I couldn't make it as a "southern lady" and my agitation at wanting to date girls rather than boys.

In stage two, mid-adolescents begin to have clearer sexual thoughts and arousal. This can result in a kind of disorientation for those youth who are isolated during this process.

> They also have internalized widespread misconceptions about homosexuality (e.g. Gay males are effeminate. Lesbians hate men). However, the need to hide inhibits many young people from asking questions and blocks access to other gay people. Inability to identify with widespread stereotypes and lack of access to openly gay adult role models, who can foster healthy, integrated lives, result in identity confusion and cognitive dissonance—a sense that what one feels or perceives is out of step with the perceptions of others. . . . When heterosexual peers are developing communication and self-disclosure skills that enhance ability to interact and form intimate relationships, lesbian and gay youth are learning how to hide core aspects of identity.[5]

Again, I have seen the effects of this stage wreak havoc on youth and adults who remain stuck here. For example, I have known several very bright students who went from straight A's to barely getting by or dropping out of school altogether. I have witnessed youth pick up drugs or alcohol at this point in an attempt to numb both their sexual urges and the pain of social isolation. I have sat with adults frustrated by their limited communication and relationship skills. While their adolescent peers were practicing and gaining these competencies, many gay, lesbian, bisexual, and transgender young adults were shutting down emotionally. Thus, sometime later they have to catch up on skills and experiences previously missed. Usually, the toll taken is much heavier than had they had this chance as teenagers.

In stage three, Troidan says that youth begin to self-identify and come out to other g/l/b/t peers. While they may pass as heterosexual in most settings, they have begun to explore and express their sexual orientation more honestly in some settings, especially those perceived by the individual as safe. As a stage in the process, this moment may grant some much needed time and space. Youth can practice their coming out and coping skills and create a support system, without being faced by the fire of oppression everywhere they go. However, as in previous stages, the risk is remaining here too long, separating sexual and social identities, acting one way in public and another in private. This can lead to risky sexual acting out or unhealthy relationship patterns. Again, as a psychotherapist, I have sat with many adults of all ages stuck in this adolescent stage of development. For example, to the world someone appears to be a happily married father of three children. However, at night he is on the Internet, arranging sexual rendezvous with unknown male partners. Then there is the lesbian so afraid her mother will find out that she won't even come out to her physician upon the discovery of a lump in her breast. Thus, her life partner is left in the waiting room during the discussion of treatment. Enabling adolescents to move through these stages appropriately could prevent these adult conflicts from occurring.

Stage four manifests self-acceptance and identity integration. In other words, people have negotiated their path through the previous tasks and steps, making their way to the other side of this process. By this point, someone has generally come out in most times and places of life. The felt need to hide is gone and disclosure is normal. As Michael Signorellie describes in his book *Outing Yourself,* one is basically out without giving it much thought. One is simply him- or herself, wherever he or she may be.

The harassment inflicted upon youth and young adults who are perceived to be gay, lesbian, bisexual, or transgender is not the only result of more exposure. Visibility can also mean connection and information. Gay, lesbian, bisexual, transgender, and questioning youth can find one another on the Internet, at the gay/straight school alliance, in the coffee shop, and attending some churches. Kids can find healthy out adult role models and friends as never before. They have the chance to what teenagers ought to do—hang out with friends, practice the ins and outs of dating, dream about the great contributions they are going to make to the world, and enjoy themselves.

During the past decade, social and support groups for gay, lesbian, bisexual, transgender, and questioning youth have sprung up across the country. Six years ago my life partner and I were asked to chaperone the first Concord Outright youth dance in the area. Along with several other gay and lesbian adult couples, we moved around the dance floor with the ease of familiarity. However, we were a little disturbed that the youth spent most of the night dancing in opposite gender couples. As a chaperone I remember thinking that I would have preferred to sit down and catch up on conversation with adult friends, but felt for some unknown reason that it was important to keep dancing. Finally by the end of the night, youth were dancing with same gender partners and looking more comfortable with one another. The next day when I saw a young lesbian who had been there I asked her, "Hey, what was up? How come it was the end of the night before girls started dancing with girls and boys with boys?" She looked down at the ground and said, "Just because we're starting to come out younger doesn't mean we have it all together. That was the first time I've seen any same-sex couples dance together. I wanted to watch you guys before I jumped in."

Over time in my practice in psychotherapy, I have received phone calls from panicked parents. "My son just came out to me. I want to support him. I want him to get what he needs. Can he come talk to you?" "Does he want to come talk to me?" I ask. So far the answer has always been, "Yes." He/she wants to talk with someone who understands. Respect, information, visibility, connection, and meaningful relationship with others are what gay, lesbian, bisexual, transgender, and questioning youth and

relational y.min.

young adults need. Clearly, these needs are no different from those of the rest of us, whatever our age and orientation.

TIMOTHY

Like Leanne, I have read much of the academic research in journals and books dealing with g/l/b/t issues as they pertain to youth and young adults. I have bookcases filled with books, and file drawers filled with articles. Being informed is as important as having had my own experiences. Among all this research, however, there is a startling lack of information about the role that religion and faith play in the lives of g/l/b/t folk. While some excellent counseling materials include sexual orientation and gender identity issues, they rarely discuss the factor of faith traditions and religion. The issue simply has not been adequately addressed.

For many lesbian, gay, bisexual, transgender, and questioning youth and young adults, faith journeys and coming-out journeys are inextricably bound together, wound around each other in unique ways that are significantly different from the faith journeys and sexuality journeys of their heterosexual peers. Transgender youth and young adults also have a special journey vis-à-vis their peers who are not questioning their gender identities, whose biology corresponds to their gender identity.

Often, the intersection of these two journeys is a painful one, wrought with struggle and conflict so great that the two journeys must be undertaken separately, or one forsaken for the other. Some choose to continue their faith journey, and arrest their coming-out journey. These youth and young adults are devout folks, heavily invested in their faith communities. However, they often speak of feeling incomplete, of not being whole, of not having integrity. Some of the stories in this collection reflect this type of journey in a basic way.

More often, though, it is the faith journey that is arrested and the coming-out journey that is pursued. When this occurs, it has often followed an intensely devout period, but the faith aspects of the person's life are rejected, intentionally cast aside, maybe forgotten, but also often resented. Rejection of a faith tradition, just as suppression of one's orientation or identity, can render a young person incomplete, unwhole, without integrity. Some of the stories in this collection reflect this other type of journey as well.

For other youth and young adults, the faith journey and the coming-out journey are not separated but are simultaneously pursued. Sometimes this leads to a duality of existence, where one's faith is a separate reality that never comes into contact with one's affectional orientation or gender identity. This, too, is a type of lack of integration. Some of the stories reflect this type of journey.

There are also youth and young adults whose faith journeys and coming-out journeys are simultaneously pursued and fully integrated. These young people have yet another type of experience, and are fortunate not to have experienced life as incomplete, unwhole, or without integrity, since their sexual orientation or gender identity and their faith have continued to be woven together. Some of the stories reflect this last basic type of journey.

It seems to me that the suffering and suicidal script by which many queer youth and young adults have led their lives is due to this separation, this lack of integration of their particular faith traditions and their sexual orientation or gender identity. It also seems to me that this suffering and suicidal script is often the only one that is seen by queer young people, that few healthy scripts have been lived out as examples of which they are aware. It is not my intention to disavow the realness of the pain of anyone's journey. It is, however, our intention to offer through the medium of this collection stories of all sorts that are lifted up both to point out the realness of the pain, and to point out that it need not be the only path.

I hope that the youth and young adults whose faith journeys and sexuality or gender identity journeys are becoming separated will herein find some kernel that resonates strongly with them. These two life experiences need not be discongruous, as my experience was, but can be whole.

Defined by God's Grace

Developmental Dynamics of Faith

I had an accepting pastor that I was able to talk to but she left. I have a hard time relating to the new pastor. I went to a Christian college. They tried to change me, so I've moved on. (20-year-old gay man)

If we had rejected our son, we would have been accepted in our church. (Mother of a young gay man)

I came out because of and through the church. I did not find support in the secular society, but I did find it in the wider church. (21-year-old gay man)

The church isn't really important to me. It is to my parents, but it just doesn't have anything to say to me. (16-year-old bisexual woman)

The church youth group was the worst experience of my life. The pastor said that Satan was claiming my life. It was scary. He didn't know me, but he condemned me to hell. (17-year-old lesbian)

I know that I'm gay. Can I be Christian? (21-year-old lesbian)

Youth and young adults communicate to us all the time about their spirits, their spiritualities, their beliefs in and rejections of formalized religious rituals and theologies. They can speak, often quite loudly, about what they love and hate, and express great pain about their confusions and hurts. They speak with words and looks, music and art, tone and tenor of voice, dress, and behaviors. In the same way that we must each accomplish the psychological and social tasks of adolescence in order to mature into our fullest selves, we must also engage this process spiritually. Sometimes it is harder to come out of the spiritual closet than the sexual closet. Although not an easy process for anyone, it is usually much harder for gay, lesbian, bisexual, transgender, and questioning youth.

They remind us how deeply intertwined are spirituality and sexuality. In this day and age, too many of these kids are being raised within religious walls that confine and condemn before they ever get the chance to explore and affirm themselves and the God in whose image they are made. Others who are fortunate enough to be nurtured into adulthood within a Welcoming Congregation may find a place to step forth onto their spiritual/sexual journey with support and love. As quoted above, one teenager may be told that she has been overtaken by the devil, while another finds that church is the most supportive place he has found. The number of persons who are struggling to recover from harmful religious messages is staggering. Just recently, a client brought into my office a cassette tape of a religious service in which her parents had participated. During the service, lesbians were called "abominable sinners who must confess . . . not natural . . . needing conversion and support to change." We cannot stand by while our youth are forced to filter their way through messages of condemnation and shame that can haunt them through their earthly existence. As Matthew Fox writes in the forward to *Coming Out Spiritually* by Christian de la Huerta:

> The God of homophobia is a mistaken God, one that hates part of the Divine creation. Such an image of God

will not last. To worship such a God is to blaspheme the God of creation. . . . Learn to love yourself, however you have been created. It is all a glorious creation, a making in God's image.[1]

There are many ways to understand and approach the process by which we come to know ourselves as persons of faith, or of faithing ourselves into connections with ultimate meaning, beauty, and spirit. In his book, *Will Our Children Have Faith?* John H. Westerhoff defines faith as a verb, as a way "of knowing, being, and willing." He then writes of what he describes as "four styles of faith—experienced faith, affiliative faith, searching faith, and owned faith."[2] These four styles of faith provide a helpful model to understand the process that g/l/b/t and questioning youth and young adults must pass through in order to claim themselves as fully sexual and spiritual beings.

The first style of faith is that of experienced faith. At its simplest, experienced faith means exactly what is says. We learn about religious faith by the ways in which it is lived around us. It is about actions, and then about how actions associated with words provide meaning, interpretation, and vocabulary to our faith.

> Experience is foundational to faith. A person first learns Christ not as a theological affirmation but as an affective experience. . . . It is not so much the words we hear spoken that matter most, but the experiences we have which are connected to those words. . . . If a person is abused whenever the word love is spoken, the word love takes on a new meaning for the person. A new definition can be learned, but the power of the word will be related to the experiences of the word.[3]

No matter our age, a positive experience of the community of faith happens when we are welcomed, attended to, and cared for. Likewise, a negative experience occurs when we are overlooked or turned away. A damaging blow to the soul can occur when the spoken words and the lived experience of those around us are counter to our own.

When I was a young child I loved church. The people were friendly and warm. Adults knew me by name and regularly spoke to me. The snacks were always more special than what we had at home. I got to perform in plays and choirs and participate in strange and mysterious rituals. However, whenever words like "love," "marriage," or "family" were used, they were always associated with heterosexual units. There were no other verbal, visual, or experienced options.

Thus, as a young teen I felt crazy. The world inside my head and the world of my experienced faith were completely disconnected. I think of the client sitting in my office as we listen to the tape her parents sent her of a worship service in which lesbians were referred to as abominable sinners, while also hearing words like love, peace, eternal life, joy, and fellowship. One can only imagine the emotional and spiritual damage done to the other young lesbian, gay, bisexual, transgender, and questioning children and adolescents sitting there with their families. As Marilyn Alexander and James Preston write in their book *We Were Baptized Too: Claiming God's Grace for Lesbians and Gays,* the church is baptizing lesbian/gay/bisexual/transgender babies all the time. They are also sitting in the pews and Sunday school rooms being damaged or affirmed by the style of their experienced faith.

Perhaps one of the most profound experiences of healing I have ever sat through in church occurred two years ago. As I sat with my partner and our children in our regular pew during worship, two lesbian couples and their infants stepped forth for the sacrament of baptism. Although I had officiated at the baptisms and naming ceremonies of several children of lesbians, I had never witnessed anyone else in this role. Neither had my children. They were captivated. I had never seen them pay such close attention in church! Their experience prior to this had been like my own—baptism in traditional churches is either for straight families, or Mom does it. The experience of this ritual healed what had gone before.

The second style of faith Westerhoff names as affiliative faith. In this style of faithing, persons come to know the powerful effects of belonging, of sensing home with others, of ritual, history, and art that speak to connection and community. Building upon one's early experience, affiliative faith calls to us and claims us as part of a larger whole, an essential ingredient. Through the experience of affiliative faith, we learn that we are not alone, that we are set apart because we are connected. Again, the power in this moment of faith is that it can be profoundly healing or damaging. Developmentally, this is a time when children and youth claim the values of their parents and elders: "This is who we are." The need to belong runs deep. So what happens if the values espoused and taught by those to whom you are the closest set you apart into exile, diminish, or condemn you? How many adolescents have been cut to the core by words like "faggot" or "queer"? How many have been harmed by the heterosexual dating and marriage rituals presented as their only option? How many have felt their feelings of difference glaringly obvious when no nonheterosexual role models are presented that they can identify with and look up to?

I cannot recount how many youth and young adults have described to me their experiences of serving as church and school leaders, going through the motions with the phrase, "If they only knew" ringing in the back of their minds. The message they have internalized is that gay, lesbian, bisexual, and transgender persons are not welcome here, do not belong, and are not part of the affiliative community of faith, no matter how successful or good they may be. They learn this not only by the presence of negative messages, but by the absence of positive ones. Thus, youth and adults feel forced into choosing between losses—"Do I come out and lose my community or stay closeted and lose myself?" It is at this point that many g/l/b/t youth and young adults walk way from the church, as one person stated, believing it is irrelevant at best and stupid at worst.

The harmful effects of a heterosexist community of faith are obvious in this stage of affiliative faith. Conversely, the healing results of a diverse and inclusive community are powerful. The yearly gathering of the United Church of Christ Coalition of Lesbian, Gay, Bisexual, and Transgender Concerns and other denominational support groups serve as lifelines of affiliation. To belong sexually/spiritually in worship, as a whole being, without leaving parts of oneself at the door of the sanctuary, is truly sacred and still rare for many. Recently I was asked to speak to a group of student leaders at an area prep school. Throughout the course of our conversation, several students expressed very positive views about diversity in sexual orientation and gender identity, which they had learned from their families and Welcoming Congregations back home.

About halfway into the evening a young man came out as questioning his own sexual orientation. He was met with respect and support by his peers—a profound moment of affiliative faith and belonging. The message was clear, "We are a community that supports and encourages you—whatever your sexual orientation."

The third style of faith described by Westerhoff is that of searching faith. Perhaps more than any other period in religious life, this one clearly aligns with adolescent development. In families, teenagers are always stepping out on their own, questioning everything their parents say and do. Parents are always having to remind themselves that teens have to get mad at you or they would never leave! The same is true with questions of religion and spirituality. In order to grow into a mature faith, one has to question and experiment.

Youth ask direct and difficult questions of adults, and they demand answers. Unfortunately, this often makes adults in institutions such as church anxious and worried. So kids leave, muttering under their breath how stupid church is. I have met many adults whose understanding of Christianity stopped at this stage. Their adult beliefs are limited by their childhood church's lack of tolerance and expansion. Thus, when they learn about the Welcoming Church movement and gay/lesbian/bisexual/ transgender positive theologies, they can hardly believe it. If they are willing to continue the searching style of faith, they may journey their way back home, into a fully owned and renewed faith experience.

The final style of faith that Westerhoff describes is that of owned faith. When persons reach this style, they strive to limit any dissonance between their words and deeds. They step out of the spiritual and sexual closet. They stand up for themselves and their beliefs. Essentially, they come out spiritually. For gay/lesbian/bisexual/transgender persons of faith this often involves loss and letting go, as well as claiming and reclaiming. It is a process of death and resurrection. I think of the twenty-year-old lesbian who left her family church in which she had been a "favored daughter" because she knew the church's position on homosexuality.

For two years, she did not enter a church building, although she missed it terribly. Once she felt strong in her sexual identity, she began to look for a congregation that would affirm her. She found one and is a very active member in it. At present, she is considering whether to go to seminary or social work school. I think of the young gay man, who will not attend church with his family since the pastor condemned homosexuality from the pulpit. He used to be the president of the youth group. Now he is active with a Wiccan community. I think of g/l/b/t young adults who are volunteering in towns and cities across the country helping youth through support groups, social events, suicide prevention programs, and gay/straight school alliances. As Christian de la Huerta writes, "I see a wave . . . sweeping across this country . . . of lavender light, a wave of beauty, a wave of creativity, a wave of selfless service, compassion, and generosity . . . a wave of Spirit . . ."[4] Tolanda Henderson, a young African-American lesbian, said to a roomful of mostly white and mostly adult persons at the UCC Coalition for Lesbian, Gay, Bisexual, and Transgender Concerns that the power of an atom is in the electron. It is not in the middle—it is on the edge. Gay, lesbian, bisexual, transgender, and questioning youth and young adults comprise that spiritual and sexual power at the edge. They are energy and passion, creativity and vision. Yet, they still need connection to the center in order to not spin off and burn out. The hope and prayer of this book is to affirm what one writer says—that all gay, lesbian, bisexual, transgender, and questioning youth and young adults will know themselves as defined by the grace of God in their lives, and not by their sexual orientation.

Part One

SHARING
OUR
STORIES

Leanne

When I was a teenager I thought I was crazy, really crazy. I needed this book. According to my family, church, and society, I probably was crazy. They needed this book too. I grew up surrounded by huge magnolia trees, white columned porches, polite gentility, and rigid, though often unspoken, rules and expectations. There was a lot to love in my life as a child— lying on the ground imagining the earth spinning on its axis while creating designs in the clouds; setting up miniature golf courses in the back yard with my brothers and their friends; Saturday evening barbeques with my parents followed by Sunday morning church. Yet, something was wrong, something was off, and I wondered if anyone knew besides me. I could never become the "southern lady" for which I was being groomed. I was neither interested nor able. As the years went by from childhood into adolescence, the darkness, panic, despair, and isolation grew.

During the summer of 1970, when I was turning thirteen, I went on a trip with my best friend, Alice. It was a great adventure. She and I, with two suitcases and my guitar, hopped on a greyhound bus, heading for east Tennessee to spend a week with her grandmother. On the ride I pulled out my guitar and, with the total abandon of youth, we played and sang our way across the state. It was invigorating, exciting, ecstatic. It was the perfect time. Alice and I spent the days walking down dirt roads, telling stories, singing songs, and trying, unsuccessfully, to smoke Swisher Sweets. I loved having all this time alone with my friend. I was in love, as only young teens can be.

One morning while walking through the living room, I noticed a magazine laying on top of the coffee table. The lead article was printed in bold across the cover—"Coming to Terms with My Lesbian Daughter: A Mother's Story." I was struck frozen, unable to move or breathe, afraid Alice or her grandmother would march out of the kitchen to catch me in my fascination, shame, and secret. Then my life would be ruined forever. Quickly and quietly, I tiptoed over to the table, picked up the magazine, rolled it up under my shirt, and went into the bathroom, locking the door behind me. Trying to breathe normally, I sat down on the edge of the tub and opened the magazine. Hearing my own heart pound out loud I first skimmed it, and then slowly and carefully digested every single word. I sneaked the magazine upstairs and into my suitcase. I went back home a transformed person.

Suddenly, life became simpler and more complicated at the same time. There was a name for people like me—"lesbian." I knew it was supposed to be disgusting. I knew that I should be ashamed, just like I was supposed to feel about the other words that I began to connect with—gay/queer/butch/fag/dyke. They were supposed to be shameful, but for me they rang true. Yes, my life was simpler. I knew who I was. I began to understand why I felt so different, so lonely, so afraid, and yet so hopeful at the same time. Obviously, there were others like me somewhere. This was a real thing. Maybe I wasn't so crazy after all. Simple. Yet this truth brought with it another whole layer of complications. Now, every homophobic joke, comment, or gesture cut to the core of my heart.

My friendship with Alice became confusing. I felt guilty without knowing why and without doing anything wrong. So, I backed off, as I did with all of my relationships at home, at school, and at church. I spent more time alone, a sullen teen in my room with a guitar. I wrote love songs to real and imaginary girlfriends. I dreamed, prayed, wished, and raged that the world would be different.

On Sunday nights after church youth group meetings, I yearned for some quiet space. I was trying to contain my panic and the growing darkness inside while other kids were goofing around waiting for rides home. With the weekly pit in my stomach alerting me that Monday morning was coming yet again, I sneaked off into the sanctuary. Quietly making my way up the stairs of the church, again hoping that no one would catch me in my fascination, shame, and secret, I opened a door. Crossing over from the hallway into the sanctuary, I felt as if I could breathe, as if I could push away all those teenage flirtations and expectations, as if I could silence the voices of culture screaming out what is and isn't acceptable for southern girls. I felt so alone. I felt so frightened. I dreamed about the relief of death and landing in the arms of a loving God. I fantasized about the excitement of life and landing in the arms of a beautiful woman. I begged God to let me meet someone else like me, someone who would love and understand me and perhaps teach me to love and understand myself. I survived, barely.

As junior high turned into high school, I fantasized blurting out, "I WANT TO DATE GIRLS." Standing in the kitchen at home, sitting through classes at school, and worshiping in the sanctuary at church I panicked, "What would they do to me if they knew?" Like many gay, lesbian, bisexual, transgender, and questioning youth then and now, I drank too much, smoked too much, and engaged in self-harming behaviors as a misguided attempt to address the pain of isolation and the trauma of oppression. Sometimes I imagined killing myself, and a few times I made gestures.

Once on a youth mission trip I swallowed too many aspirin. A friend found me crying on the back steps of our cabin. He told the youth minister, who took me to the hospital. I'm sure I didn't want to die, but I knew no words to express the pain inside. I needed help, but the truth of my pain remained closeted for many years to come. In fact, I was twenty years old before

I told anyone I was a lesbian. Being a teenager was horrible for me. I felt dishonest, ashamed, and enraged—abandoned by my culture, my family, and my church. Even so, I remained deeply religious. My belief in God kept me alive. *mmm...*

Decades later, I am amazed and thankful that I am alive, that I made it through this most torturous time of coming of age and coming to terms. How did I do it? I am smart enough to know that I did not do it on my own. A combination of people and experiences worked together on my behalf, even without my own awareness. God's Holy Spirit hovered close. I know now that the essence of faith that was transmitted to me was *Yay!* strong enough to overcome the legalistic interpretations of scripture and social mores of homophobia. Certainly, like many gay/lesbian/bisexual/transgender youth and adults, I channeled my sexual energy in other directions. I was always busy, always doing something "respectable" at church or school. I often had boyfriends who were genuinely good friends and wonderful covers for my true affections.

Perhaps the hardest part of being a closeted and isolated lesbian teen was the double identity that I maintained. Often, I felt like two separate people trapped inside one body. The "good girl" was the school student body president, conference and local church youth leader, and basketball player who held down a part-time job and kept good grades. The "social deviant" fantasized about girls, hid away in my room smoking cigarettes, giving voice to my pain through music for no one's ears but my own. Sometimes in an effort to bring together the southern lady and the social deviant I would sneak away with a boy or two, get drunk, and try to enjoy flirting or making out. It didn't work. In my acting out, I continued to feel like a split personality, and I became more sure than ever that I was a lesbian.

At age twenty, I first spoke the word lesbian out loud to another human being. As I began to connect with other gay and lesbian friends, I found I had to disconnect with the church. I quit my job as a youth minister, changed my plan of attending seminary, and detoured instead to social work school. I'm not sure whether I left the church out of the sense of shame or the need to survive. Nonetheless, I believed that I could not come out as a healthy young lesbian while deeply involved in my church. The paradox here is that the coming-out process was one of the most spiritual events of my life, yet it could only take place outside the bounds of the religious community. Eventually, however, I returned to the church. I went to seminary, moved to New England, and joined the United Church of Christ in which I am still a minister in good standing. I continue to be actively involved in the Open and Affirming movement and the Coalition for Lesbian, Gay, Bisexual, and Transgender Concerns. As much as I am intimately connected to church, I am still an outsider to many. Nonetheless, I no longer believe that I have to disconnect from the church in its entirety to live as a healthy self-identified lesbian. My life's prayer is that no one will ever again feel forced to leave his/her faith community in order to affirm him/herself as a beloved child made in the image and likeness of God.

4

Timothy

As a teenager, my faith journey became very separate from my coming out journey, needlessly so. I share some of it here, omitting the names of particular congregations and individuals; there are readers who will recognize them without the names, but the omissions are intentional to prevent the appearance of condemning, which might stand in the way of reaping the full benefits of this collection for some.

My sister and I were baptized in a United Methodist church on Easter Sunday, 1968. It was the church in which my mother had grown up, and where my parents were married. We attended that church when I was very small. Eventually, the family moved to my father's hometown. My father's family had left an unaffiliated Baptist church for a Congregational Christian (now United Church of Christ) church in the 1950s; in spite of this, we attended that unaffiliated Baptist church for a couple of years until the United Church of Christ began a Sunday school program. I recall as a first-grader in that Baptist Sunday school crying great tears because I was the only one who was not "saved."

One of my first memories in that UCC church was playing the part of Joseph in the Christmas pageant. I didn't have any lines; I just had to stand there and admire the baby. That was Christmas 1972. I sang in the children's choir, then as we grew older the youth choir. In high school, a friend and I played taps on our trumpets outside on Memorial Day services. After I had enough piano lessons, my mother, who had become the keyboardist, decided I could play an offertory and the doxology one Sunday. Thus began many years of involvement as a church musician.

Interestingly enough, what I recall as one of my first exposures to lesbian/gay issues came from my father after church. It was Easter Sunday; I was probably ten or eleven. In the church bulletin, I noticed that my grandmother had given flowers in memory of a woman whose surname I recognized as my grandmother's maiden name. I asked my father who she was, and he told me she was our cousin. I asked why I'd never heard of her before, and he said that it was because she was a lesbian. I didn't know what a lesbian was and so, of course, I asked about that too. He revealed his own understanding at the time, telling me that lesbians are woman who have something wrong with them, liking other women instead of men and really wanting to be men. In our cousin's case, he explained, she had a woman friend, instead of a man friend. He even stated that our cousin had more wrong with her than her friend, because our cousin drove the tractor outside and mowed the lawn, doing "man" things, while the friend stayed inside and cooked and cleaned, doing "girl" things. I thought about this conversation as an adolescent struggling with my own sexual orientation, and thought that something must be wrong with me as well.

By the time I was in high school, I became the regular church organist, while my mother served as the substitute. Around this time, I began to recognize my attraction to members of the same gender. It was a very confusing thing, and certainly not one I was willing to share with anyone, certainly not my father and certainly not the pastor. It would have been far too risky. (I've since learned that the pastor would have been fine to tell.) I remember casually flipping through Leviticus one day about age sixteen, and being filled with horror that I was a disgusting abomination to God. There were other verses on homosexuality there in the Bible, at least according to the index for my King James Version. So I read them. I wanted God to change me. Nothing happened, though, and my faith journey continued while my coming to terms with my sexuality stopped. While I rarely admit this, at the time I felt what some would term a call from God.

After high school, I went off to college to major in music at the State University of New York College at Fredonia, and became involved in a nearby UCC church there. I was even the choir director for a short time. During this same time, my faith journey continued, or rather narrowed, as I became a near fundamentalist. This was not the result of attending either UCC church but because that mentality was a safe space in which to hide while struggling with affectional orientation issues. I do not recall hearing any homophobic remarks from any UCC pulpit; but neither was anything positive ever articulated.

During this period, I interestingly acquired a fascination for apocryphal, noncanonical texts. I have continued to study these as an adult. The struggle between my faith and my orientation eventually grew too much for me. I could not integrate my orientation with my faith. When I acquired a girlfriend, and when that relationship became physical, the struggle became all the more difficult. I didn't feel right. I church-hopped a little (still calling it "being ecumenical") and found intellectual challenges with the Unitarian Universalists. They seemed safe enough, and didn't really condemn anyone.

So in 1985, I stopped attending the UCC church near the campus. The great irony is that the General Synod of the United Church of Christ passed an Open and Affirming resolution that same year. I continued, however, to play or direct as a substitute in whatever denomination needed someone, Lutheran, Methodist, or whatever, and continued to play when I was home. At one point, I played in a Unitarian Universalist Church for several months. That was the same semester I officially "came out." I noticed that the Unitarians had gone to the trouble of making a brochure about gay rights, and that they had no problem putting this right out on display at the church. I then began to wonder if it might be possible that one could be a person of faith *and* gay. However, my faith journey continued to be arrested.

Like so many other g/l/b/t and questioning youth and young adults, I didn't know where to meet people and went to the sparsely attended gay student group on campus. I also went to bars.

After graduation from college, I attended Unitarian Universalist churches almost exclusively. They had, after all, specifically stated that I was welcome. I continued to be unaware of the United Church of Christ denominational position. Somewhere along the way, I began to identify as agnostic, or sometimes even atheist; it seemed the path of least resistance. Ironically, though, I continued to attend church.

But I still didn't really know where to meet people, and continued to go to bars. The people I met there were not for the most part healthy role models, following their own suffering and suicidal scripts, seeming more interested in alcohol and casual sex than in meaningful relationships and thought. Since I was not interested in either, I felt very isolated. One night in June of 1988 I was assaulted in Rochester, New York, while leaving a gay bar alone. Acid was sprayed in my face. I'm not sure how I managed to get away, but I did, and spent the night at the emergency room. My left contact lens dissolved in my eye. I felt very fortunate a week later when the patch came off and I could see. Not being able to wear contact lenses for a few months seemed a small price to pay.

Leaping ahead a few years, after graduate school, I obtained a position as a music director in a United Methodist Church. A national board member of Affirmation, the United Methodist lesbian/gay group, was a member of that congregation. I was happy to learn this, and remembered that Unitarian brochure from several years before. I wondered when Methodists would make such a brochure. Through my friend's influence, I attended a national Affirmation meeting and became aware that years before the UCC had passed its Open and Affirming resolution.

It still seems odd to have learned this from someone outside the denomination.

Leaping ahead again several years, the United Methodist church choir I direct (a different one than in the previous paragraph) participated in the opening worship of the 1996 General Conference. It was here that I as a young adult had a very painful experience. Affirmation is not a recognized group of the denomination; neither is the Reconciling Congregation Program. They were not allowed booths in the exhibition hall. The United Methodist *Book of Discipline* has several antigay paragraphs in it; in spite of all the activities and efforts of the Reconciling Congregation Program, the delegates voted to add further restrictions, prohibiting United Methodist clergy from performing same-gender unions or from allowing them to happen in United Methodist facilities. When the vote was counted, I felt as if the several thousand delegates had slapped me simultaneously. It was a clear statement of unwelcome. Since I have never joined a United Methodist Church, my journey out of the pain was to explore what the other possibilities might be. I recognized that if I pursued a United Methodist faith journey I would not be able to continue with integrity on my journey as a gay man.

It was at this time that I began to attend a local United Church of Christ congregation—an Open and Affirming one. This began the reintegration of my faith journey and my affectional orientation (just as my "official" status as a young adult was ending). The following year I knew I had made the right decision for me when I attended the UCC General Synod. The choir of the United Church Coalition for Lesbian/Gay Concerns (its name at the time) had been invited to sing at the opening worship ceremony. There were booths in the exhibition hall for the Coalition, for the Opening and Affirming Program, for UCC Parents of Lesbians and Gays, and even for a project of the United Church Board for Homeland Ministries called "Equal Rights in Covenant Life," dealing with same-gender unions. Resolutions dealing with same-gender unions were overwhelmingly voted positively. Not to put United Methodism down, but for me the contrast between the two denominational meetings was extraordinary. The integrity I feel now is much healthier. Since I spend less energy on one integrated, whole-person journey than on two journeys that alternate being arrested or pursued, I have also been able to respond to the tapping on my shoulder.

I'm glad to be back in my community of origin. It has become my community of choice. I am now a Commissioned Minister of the United Church of Christ, serving as the Youth and Young Adult Program Coordinator for the United Church of Christ Coalition for Lesbian, Gay, Bisexual, and Transgender Concerns.

Part Two

IN OUR OWN VOICES

Stories of Harm, Healing, and Hope

If we wait until we are not afraid to speak,
we will be speaking from our graves.

— Audre Lorde

Anne

Unconditional Love (Clause 12b)

Of course I still love (ew, that's just unnatural).
Of course I'm not ashamed. It's not my fault.
We raised you right.
But hey baby, didn't you read the contract?
And I quote: "I will love and support you always and forever."
Unless you politically or sexually deviate.
Call your lawyer to verify.
In the meantime, get out of my house, faggot.

Amanda

I grew up in the church and always believed it would be an important part of my life. When I was young I had an incredibly strong belief in God and I wanted the spirit to work through me to reach others. Over time I would come to realize that my involvement within the church had a prerequisite—I had to be straight.

I knew from a very young age that I was different than the majority of other people. Many have looked at me incredulously when I tell them that I can remember having a same-sex crush when I was only four. They say that because I was so young I couldn't possibly have already been noticing my attraction for other females. However, they don't seem to find it hard to believe that my three-year-old cousin, Tim, has a crush on his next door neighbor Becky. No matter how young you are, heterosexuality is easy to believe. Why isn't the opposite true? Even now some tell me that I am too young to know what my orientation is. Again, they don't question the heterosexual orientation of my brother, who is a full five years younger than me.

My parents faithfully brought me to their small-town Methodist congregation every week when I was young. I learned many things within this church community. They taught me love and thanksgiving; they also taught me fear and shame. It almost seems as if the inward struggle between my church and my sexuality was always there. The services lifted my spirit and moved me to act for God, but later they sent the message that I was sinful and disgusting. The more I became aware of my same-sex attraction the more I began to loathe myself. Religiously, I had been taught that I must not have enough faith in God or I wouldn't be tempted by Satan in this way. For three years I think I took "pray without ceasing" to its most literal. I prayed continually for God to release me from my sins. I asked for forgiveness daily for my "impure" thoughts. I went to church several times a week so that they could not say my faith wasn't strong enough. The more homosexuality was brought up in church, the worse I felt about myself. I never heard one good thing about those "queers" when I was young. In church I never heard anything but hate and anger towards them. It was made very clear from a young age that being gay was a terrible thing.

It didn't help that my crush when I was four was for the church nursery attendant. Perhaps it should have comforted me that it was someone within the congregation. She was strong and beautiful, and I was in awe of her. It amazes me now how early we learn shame. At that young age I had no idea what the word homosexual meant, but I knew that what I was feeling was not something to be celebrated. I remember feeling constant shame for the way I dressed, the toys I played with, and the kids I hung out with. Later that shame would be multiplied because of my feelings for other females. Children learn at an incredibly young age what mold they are supposed to fit into. I always played with boys, preferring their trucks and action figures to playing house and Barbies. Even the most well meaning of church members would nag at me to try playing with dolls or wearing dresses. It was hurtful to know that I didn't act the way I was supposed to.

As I got older my same-sex attraction only grew. I loved God and was very active within my church. The message that I could not be both gay and Christian was clear. I began hiding huge parts of myself so that people wouldn't discover my terrible secret. I buried my homosexual feelings deep inside, refusing to even acknowledge them myself. I played the part of the good heterosexual Christian girl. I dated guys and talked end-lessly about the boys I had crushes on. Only it was all a facade. I never felt anything with any of the guys I dated and only talked so much about them to keep people from suspecting what I had long feared. I actually thought that if I tried hard enough to be straight, eventually my efforts would pay off.

Then I met Jane. She had also grown up in the church but we had never really gotten to know each other until we were in the same Sunday school class in junior high. She and I spent hours together planning events for the church. I had finally met someone who loved God as much as I did. Slowly our friend-ship evolved into more. It became clear that we both had feel-ings for one another. We fought those feelings for a very long time before we gave in to them because we had both been taught that it was wrong. I will never forget how I felt the first time she kissed me. It was like suddenly the whole world felt right and this was the most natural evolution of our close friendship. This was the thing that the minister said was disgusting? It didn't feel that way to me. In fact it felt very clean and good and spiritual.

If only I had been able to hold on to those feelings. After Jane left that day all I could think about was how I was dis-obeying everything I had been taught. All of the sermons kept coming back to me—sick, disgusting, sinful, a disease, an ad-diction. I shook with fear, crying for forgiveness. I felt like I had just condemned myself to hell. I avoided Jane for several days after that, scared of what might happen. I felt so much conflict. On the one hand I felt these incredibly wonderful feelings for her, while on the other I felt that I had failed God and was going to die for my sins.

Jane and I couldn't seem to stay away from each other for long, though. After only a few days apart we both confessed that we had missed the other terribly. Our friendship continued and we very slowly became physical with each other. We were so respectful of the other's boundaries that it was beautiful. We went slowly and made sure that we were both comfortable with everything. While being intimate, we had an amazing ability to talk through what we were feeling and what we wanted. However, when we weren't being sexual we didn't ever acknowledge the things that happened between us. If we had talked about it, it would have meant that we would have to face it. Facing it would be admitting that we were doing what we had always been told was wrong.

The more time we spent together the stronger our bond became, and it wasn't long before the congregation became suspicious of our friendship. We had to meet with the pastor to discuss our "problem." The pastor was very direct about how we had failed him and God. He told me that I had to step down as Youth Christian Leader. That meeting was one of the most painful things I can remember. He gave us the name of Bill, the music minister, and told us we needed to begin meeting with him on a regular basis if we intended to become right in the Lord's eyes. Bill wasn't as direct as the pastor, but he was just as painful. He told us he could "save" us if we were willing to work for it. He preached on what real love is and encouraged us to spend time apart. He even suggested to me that I go shopping for some dresses and clips for my hair. He was very insistent and he scared me.

I ran from Bill because he made it clear that just leaving Jane wasn't good enough. I would have to change my whole life. Jane clung to him and he told her lies about me. She and I were torn apart by all the conflict. I saw Jane at the local convenience store the other day. She had on a dress and heels, her hair was long, and she was on Bill's arm. She looked every bit the straight girl he said she should be. There are days when I still miss her.

I no longer attend my home church because I know that I am not welcome there. I miss having a church family, but I know now that God loves me no matter what. I am finally letting go of the lies that congregation ingrained in me. I know that I have a good relationship with God and I have worked hard to get here. I am proud to be a Christian lesbian.

Ryan

The coming-out process for many gay and lesbian people is usually agonizing and painful. I like to compare it to vomiting: you know that it's coming; you dread it to no end; you try to postpone it for as long as possible; eventually you just can't hold it in any longer and you puke. Once it's out of your system, though, you feel 100 percent better. This is the exact same way I felt towards coming out to my family. In retrospect, coming out to my family was probably one of the best things that ever happened to me. Coming out was like a rebirth of my soul. I know this sounds cheesy, but it's the truth. After I came out, I was free to be exactly the person God had created me to be.

Compared to other peoples' coming-out experiences, mine was relatively easy. I attribute that to the fact that I had not been raised in a very religious environment. I have always found this to be confusing since my father was raised in a strict, Catholic household and my mother was raised in a Baptist one. I guess they could never agree on which kind of church to go to, so they decided on neither. Instead, my parents simply raised my siblings and I to believe in God and Christ and to practice good, Christian values like honesty and love.

Believing in God, Christ, heaven, etc. was satisfying for me until I reached the age of about twelve. At that point, I wasn't really thinking about my sexuality all that much, but for some reason I began to question God and God's existence. I remember my seventh-grade history teacher lecturing on Buddhism and other faiths and that made me wonder why there were so many different religions. I came to the conclusion that every civilization had made up their own god to serve as an easy explanation for their existence and that they were all too simple-minded to consider anything else. I became an ardent evolutionist over the next three years. I used to laugh at the thought of Christians wasting their time in church. I preached to my friends that there was no God or heaven and that we were just another part in the process of evolution. I had officially become detached from God and any spirituality that I had once had.

When I started sexually experimenting with my male best friend at the age of fourteen, the thought that I was participating in an "abominable sin" never once entered my mind. In fact, up until I was about fifteen, I didn't even know that being gay was thought of as a "crime against God." I did, however, feel some guilt within me after I would experiment with my friend. The guilt I felt was caused by the thought that I had become a "faggot." Eventually I overcame that guilt because it just felt right to be with another boy.

A year later, I met the boy that I would spend the next ten months with in a relationship. At this point we were both about fifteen and in the closet. Two weeks into our relationship, I decided to come out to my family. It was a few days before Thanksgiving and I was busy preparing the individual letters that I would give to my parents and siblings explaining to them how much I loved them and how I was gay. My plan was to give them the letters the day after Thanksgiving so that I wouldn't ruin the holiday. Somehow my plan blew up in my face and I ended up telling them Thanksgiving night. It was definitely the most emotional Thanksgiving I've ever had, but it was also quite successful.

The role of homosexuality in religion was never really discussed with me during the next few months. It wasn't until my boyfriend came out to his family that I realized how much Christians despised homosexuality. It was a huge shock to me to see how my boyfriend's mother tried relentlessly to make her son straight. I couldn't understand nor believe that Christians felt justified in hating homosexuality. I painfully watched my boyfriend suffer from his mother's constant pressure to be "normal." I felt so guilty that I had never been put through that kind of trauma. It seemed like there was absolutely nothing I could do for him except to tell him that it would all work out someday. Finally, I decided that if I was ever going to help his situation I needed to first become educated on the Bible. I searched the Internet for information on homosexuality in Christianity and came upon the story of Sodom and Gomorrah, as well as the other passages from the Bible that are most commonly used against homosexuals. Then I searched for any kind of gay support groups and I discovered Parents, Friends, and Family of Lesbians and Gays (PFLAG). I contacted the local PFLAG president and she invited my family and me to one of their monthly meetings. She also recommended that I contact the minister of the gay-welcoming Wesley United Methodist Church. My mother and I met with this minister shortly after that. The minister, Jan Everhart, explained to me that the Bible can be interpreted in many ways and that you can be gay and Christian at the same time.

My meeting with Jan made me reevaluate my theories on religion and God. I decided to attend a service at Wesley with my mom. I expected to feel incredibly uncomfortable and out of place. Instead, the people there made me feel right at home. I sat down and listened intently to Jan's sermon. I remember towards the end of her sermon she said, "And we are all God's children and God loves each and every one of us." At that point I felt something within me that I had never felt before. It was such a beautiful feeling, but it hit me like a ton of bricks. I realized at that miraculous moment that there was indeed a God that loved me very much. At this realization I began to cry uncontrollably.

I continued to go to that church after my enlightenment. It was a very healing experience for my mom and me to be around other people who felt the same about God as we did. Although

I don't attend that church as much as I would like to, I feel closer to God now than I ever did. After getting in touch with my spirituality, I've realized that no one can interfere with or judge my relationship with God. I also know now that God has been and always will be in my heart. I am thankful to have come to these realizations at such an early age. I wish that more of my gay peers could have these beautiful, life-saving realizations. I trust that God is love and will always be there for anyone who opens his or her heart.

8

Shawn

All of my life, since about age eight or ten, I have always thought that I was different. I had also had sexual feelings toward males, but I kept telling myself that it was just a phase that would go away. As time went on, I had a "normal" life. I dated girls and had a girlfriend in high school. But the feelings about men were still there. I had to admit it to myself. So I did. In 1999, I was sent by my church, the Presbyterian (USA), to go to our General Assembly in Charlotte, North Carolina, as a Youth Advisory Delegate to represent my presbytery. At this meeting, I approached the PLGC (Presbyterians for Lesbian and Gay Concerns), now known as MLP (More Light Presbyterians), and told them that I thought I was gay. They were very supportive, caring, and open, and answered any questions I had. They took me under their wings. They gave me information about More Light churches in the Phoenix area. They also gave me some phone numbers of people and hotlines to call. I came back to Phoenix and was still curious about what it really meant to be gay. So I sent an e-mail to my older brother and asked a couple of hypothetical questions about homosexuality and what his feelings are about gays and homosexuality. First, to my surprise, he actually responded; and second, he was very open to the subject and answered the questions in a way that made me comfortable to come out to him. So I told him that I

2

thought I was gay. To my surprise he was very accepting of me. He also told me not to tell Mom. Well, after six weeks Mom finally found out from a close friend of mine. She said the reason I was not around was because I was gay and did not know how she would handle it. That was true, but I still think there was more to it. I was afraid of being rejected. Well, she never rejected me. Recently, I finally told my dad and he said he would not reject me either. Overall, my coming-out experience has been very positive.

My current faith is still very strong and deeply rooted. I am very thankful for this because I almost turned my back on God when I admitted to myself that I was gay. If it hadn't been for my deep belief and faith, I probably would not be here to tell you my story. My church family's reaction is somewhat what I expected. They are quiet about my sexuality because only about twenty-five people in the church know I am gay. They are still coming to terms with my sexuality. As for my nuclear family— my mother, stepfather, maternal grandmother, older brother and wife, and older sister—they too are coming to terms with me being gay.

My religion and church involvement is very important to me and my family. I have been a part of the Presbyterian Church (USA) my whole life. I am afraid to say that my local church is not a Welcoming Congregation. I was born, baptized, confirmed, and involved in my church until I resigned as elder on session because of my homosexuality. My family is also very active in my church. My grandparents are charter members. My grandfather was on the first session and board of trustees. My grandmother is active in Presbyterian Women and is currently clerk of session. My mother has only been a member of one church. She is also active in Presbyterian Women and sits on the Christian education committee.

My religion has helped me and it has also made it very difficult for me to come out. It has helped as far as teaching me to be accepting of people from all walks of life. I have always been told that everyone is a child of God. People in my church do not condemn homosexuals as people, but they condemn the homosexual lifestyle. That is what made it so difficult for me to come out to my church. They have told me that they can accept me, but it is difficult for them to accept my lifestyle, which I have learned to accept about them.

My involvement in my church is definitely a lot less than what it was before I came out to the church's leadership (session, Christian education committee, and senior high advisors). I am no longer part of these leadership groups but am still very active as a member. I still tithe and recently attended a national church-wide redevelopment conference in Los Angeles, California. I have no intentions of leaving my church because I am gay. My church is and will always be a huge part of who I am as a person and Christian.

Before I came out, my image of God was a God who is loving, caring, and accepting of all people. I think my image of God has not changed. I strongly feel that God still loves and always will love me for who I am. I have a purpose for being gay and a purpose for being here on earth. My faith and spirituality have been affected by my coming-out experience, both in a very positive way. I have a stronger faith in God and feel I am more spiritual with God and the Holy Spirit. I can honestly say I sense the Holy Spirit a lot more than before. I feel I am a lot closer with God than I was before I came out. It has also brought me closer with my family and friends, both in church and outside of church. But I am not sure if I can be a person of faith and a self-affirming young gay man.

What I want people to know about g/l/b/t youth is that we are still children of God and are having a difficult time accepting ourselves; at least I did. We need support groups in our churches and synagogues. We need places where we can go to meet other g/l/b/t people and discuss what we are going through; a place where we can feel safe and secure; and a place that can help our coming-out process go a little smoother. We need to be around people who will accept us as homosexual or bisexual or transgendered persons.

Faith communities can be most helpful to g/l/b/t and questioning youth by being less condemning of g/l/b/t people in general. I know that it is almost impossible to have that. So maybe faith communities should be more accepting and realize that we are here and are not going to go away. Remember that we are still children of God and are forgiven of our sins. I strongly feel that g/l/b/t youth and questioning people are not sinners because of their sexuality and lifestyle. Faith communities should also be more willing to offer guidance, counseling, and support groups for g/l/b/t and questioning youth and adults. Questioning is very difficult. A person wonders, am I the only one? Why me? How could God do this to me? In a safe and secure faith community, free of condemnation, judgement, prejudice, and discrimination, we can help g/l/b/t and questioning youth in their coming-out process.

9

Amy

My name is Amy; sometimes I go by Dylan. I'm nineteen, I live in Maine, I'm a lesbian, and I also identify as transgendered. This is my story of God, coming out, and finally finding acceptance.

I was baptized at my family church, the Church of the Nazarene. This is where my grandma was the organ player and another grandmother had been a Sunday school teacher many years before.

When I went to visit my grandma over the summer, I'd go to church with her and listen to her play the organ. Of course, I was there for Sunday school and the service too, but I liked my grandma's music best. When I finally started visiting my dad he had me go to church with him, which was cool because it was the same church as my grandma's. I started to drift away from church when I was about ten because I had other things to do. I was too much trouble and couldn't go to my grandma's church any longer.

At the age of thirteen, I started thinking there was something wrong with me because I really lost interest in the boy next door, but man, was his sister something! I also rediscovered my faith and started attending church with my papa and grandpa. They'd pile all four of us kids into the van and we'd take a ten-minute ride down the road to church.

The pastor and his wife were good friends of my pa's. I went through the normal routine of going to Sunday school, listening to sermons, attending picnics, going to potlucks, and watching the babies. The pastor would talk about how we would be saved if we put our love and trust in Jesus. I tried so hard to pay attention but I had so much running through my head. I thought about talking to my pastor about my feelings because I trusted him and it really started to get to me, but I didn't. I chose not to talk to him because I just didn't feel like being criticized and I didn't want to go through a replay of "The Exorcist."

I stopped going to church again when my papa passed away. I was angry with God. I started thinking that this was God's way of punishing me for being gay. Well, with my faith in question and my sexuality following closely behind, I went on with life as usual but secluded more into my own little world. I figured that the church couldn't help me. Nothing and no one could help.

Three years later, I met my boyfriend Shawn. He came from a fairly religious family. They encouraged me to go back to church. This time, church was really interesting. The pastor at this church was a big Bible-preaching man. He came from the south and he really showed it. I went just about every Sunday and sat next to Shawn, holding his hand. I pretended to be happy. His dad talked to the pastor about our relationship. So one day the pastor pulled us into his office and talked about it. He kept saying that we should wait till we were out of church and stuff. He then went on to talking to me about my home life. He kept saying, "I know things aren't all that great and if there's anything you want to talk about, you can talk to me anytime." I started getting really paranoid, thinking. "Oh no. I think he knows. I'm in so much trouble." For an entire week, I kept thinking that the pastor knew. I was caught and I was in big trouble. The following Sunday, the pastor worked the whole gay discussion into his sermon. "They're disgraceful and are going to hell." This really made me not want to be in church or ever return. I stuck it out for a couple more weeks and finally broke down. I first told Shawn, who was pretty okay with it. "Well, that would explain a lot," he said. I told him that I wasn't going to go to church anymore and that we would be better off as friends. I jumped back into my hole.

When I was sixteen and a half, I met Beth. She was a real weird character—into the whole goth scene—and she was also a writer and artist. I liked her instantly. She and I fell in love. I was a big bad tough guy, or actually a soft-hearted teddy bear in disguise. It was the leather jacket that made her fall in love with me. We were together for a couple of weeks and during those weeks she encouraged me to go to church again. This time it was a Unitarian church. The minister was a woman, and the whole congregation was really open minded. I talked to the pastor a few times and discussed being gay. She was totally okay with it. She helped me realize that being gay and loving God were totally cool. I finally had found some acceptance within a faith group and also within myself.

I'm really glad I finally talked to someone within the church about being gay. I feel that coming out is a really tough thing to do, and not having the support or being afraid to talk to your pastor or a minister could make it tougher. I've had people tell me things that have tested my faith, but I never backed down from them. This has helped me grow spiritually and emotionally.

10

Tolonda

Recently, I attended Youth Sunday at the church I grew up in. I watched the high school students acting out a play they had probably written themselves and I felt sad. I had missed out on such activities because I had gone to private boarding school in high school. My mom reminded me, though, that when I had been a part of the youth group, I hadn't felt accepted by the other kids. I was never quite sure why this was the case. Maybe it was because I was black in a New England congregation; maybe it was because I was smart and outspoken. Maybe it was because my struggle with my sexuality kept me more secluded from my peers than I had realized.

I came out when I was fifteen. For several years previous, I had been struggling with my sexuality. One part of me kept saying "You're gay"; another kept saying "No, I'm not." Finally, in the middle of the night one night in my junior year, I admitted to myself that I was sexually attracted to women. It was the first in a long line of thoughts and realizations that led to my identifying as lesbian. By then, my connection to my faith was a thin thread. I had stopped going to church. The faith community at my boarding school consisted of people who were secure in their knowledge of God's love for them. There was no room for doubters like me to grow and be nurtured where we were in our faith journeys. Although I had been raised in the church, for me church was simply something you did, not something you believed in. I could recite all the famous Bible stories, but I didn't know how they related to my life. I knew the history of the church into antiquity—its policies of mission, which smacked of domination and slavery. I also believed and still believe that God had presented itself with several faces to several groups of people, that the gods of all the earth's religions are the same supreme creator, if you will. So why be loyal to Christianity? The rise of the Christian Coalition, Religious Right, and the Moral Majority in public prominence sealed my distance from the church. I didn't want to be associated with a bunch of irrational fanatics who don't agree with a woman's right to have control over her own reproduction, or who think homosexuality is enough to doom a person to hell. I could not, however, deny that there was something out there, or something within me, that was all-encompassing. I felt that whatever it was connected me to others, but I didn't know if it fit the picture of God as described by Christians. I decided to call myself an agnostic and not think about it for a while.

Oddly enough, one of the places I spent a lot of time in the fall of my freshman year of college was the chapel. The harpsichord was my new musical passion and it was housed in the chapel for temperature control. One day while studying in the basement library, I noticed the word "closet" on the front of a publication on a shelf across the room. I was sure it couldn't mean what I thought, it couldn't be a reference to the closets gay people are constantly trying to decide whether to come out of. This was a church-related magazine. Church people don't talk about gay people. Imagine my surprise when, on closer examination, I found that this was exactly what the magazine was referring to. It turned out to be a copy of *Open Hands*, a magazine published by a group of programs similar to ONA (Open and Affirming) of the UCC throughout different denominations. I devoured the contents of that issue and every subsequent issue that came into the chapel, eager to learn how others negotiated their spirituality and their sexual orientation. Little did I know I was about to find out how this was done firsthand.

The summer after my sophomore year in college, my mother was a delegate from New Hampshire to the General Synod in Columbus, Ohio. While flipping though the schedule of events both before and during Synod, she came across an announcement for the national gathering of what was then called the United Church Coalition for Lesbian and Gay Concerns. She called me at school to suggest that I attend. I dragged my heels for a while, but then decided, what the heck. I cashed my tax return to use for registration fees and went. (I always like to say that the federal government paid for me to go and hang out with a bunch of gay people for a week.) That was probably one of the best decisions I ever made. Being at National Gathering gave me a chance to interact with people who had been dealing with the issue of being both gay and Christian for a very long time. It was there that I learned that there is no thing or person, not even myself, that could separate me from the love of God.

Most importantly, I learned that I could define what being Christian meant for me. I was very relieved to find that I could disassociate myself from the viewpoint of those who claimed to be from the same faith background but were fighting to deny my existence. That summer, I realized that some of my aversion to the church in adolescence had been related to my coming-out process. Being able to acknowledge and let go of this was critical to my reconnection to the church. For me, the question hadn't been "Can I be gay even though I'm Christian," but "Can I be Christian even though I'm gay?" I am very glad to report the answer is a resounding yes. I find it ironic that my involvement with the church at both the local and national levels has been increased by my having been involved with a group of gay people, but that is exactly what happened. I have never been a member of an ONA church, but I think I would like to. Finding one with racial diversity and a strong gay community will be a challenge, but I will certainly try.

11

Kenneth

"God hates fags!" was a phrase I had heard many times during my freshman year of high school. I was not stunned by this anymore because I had been teased since my junior high years. I must admit, I did try to think myself "straight." I began to believe this and grew to dislike gay people. During my freshman year, I became very religious. Every night I would pray, and I turned to God whenever I wanted or needed something. The funny thing was, I was praying for a life I didn't want. I was told by classmates that all gays would be sent to hell. I believed it was a fact because I had no knowledge that stated otherwise. During the summer after that year, however, I finally realized that I liked boys a little more than most guys did. I thought at that time, however, that I would still marry a girl and have lots of children and a normal life. After all, "God hates fags," and I didn't want to be hated by someone to whom I had been so devoted. I continued to pray, but now I prayed for a boyfriend, and for the first time I began to understand my life. Still very closeted about myself and the feelings I had inside, I only told one person—my best friend—who later turned out to be gay herself.

Once school resumed, I heard the same old taunts from the same kids. Now, they meant something because I was gay and what they were saying about me was true. Was it possible that God hated me? Was I a sinner in God's eyes? Would I go to hell? The answer to all of those questions was "No!" I read the Bible and did other research and found the knowledge that Jesus never spoke badly about homosexuals, but rather, he taught us to love and accept our neighbor.

With a newfound need for acceptance, and the knowledge that Jesus loved me, I went looking for the best church there was. I was baptized as a Presbyterian, but for my entire life I had gone to the Church of Christ with my grandparents. My grandparents, however, made it clear that they would not accept a homosexual person. Therefore, I believed their church wouldn't either. I then began going to a Lutheran church with my best friend at that time. I met a few people and felt welcome, but the feeling did not last. Soon thereafter, I heard kids making fun of a person from their school who they believed to be gay. I then moved on to the Mormon Church. I was surrounded by many people my age, who all liked me and never said a thing against me, to my face. I soon learned, however, that many of the kids were "afraid for me" because I acted a little too "gay." I found this out and stopped going to Mormon functions. I also quickly severed many of the ties I had with those people. I lost a large group of my friends and started to become angry toward some religions.

Next, I went a nondenominational church that my family attended every Sunday. The issue of sexual orientation was never brought up, but to me their silence was no different from the disapproval of others. People from that church blindly followed what the Bible said, but most did not read any of the parts about same-sex love, or bother to realize the Bible was written many years ago.

Lastly, I went to the Catholic church but was quickly turned away from that. A friend of mine who is Catholic told me, "I don't mind that you are gay . . . I just don't like the others. It makes me sick to think about what you people do, and I can't accept them."

I soon "fell away from faith," so to speak, because I felt that all people involved in religions would not accept me, nor would they try to understand anything about me. I stopped going to church, and I gave up on praying to someone who so many felt hated me. I was religion-less, but it had been such a large part of my life for so long that without it I felt a void.

I soon turned toward Wicca, a neopagan religion that a few of my friends believed in. Reading up on the subject for many months before ever considering myself a Wiccan, I learned that Wicca is very similar to the Christian religions I had for so long strived to fit into. They believe in a "heaven" of sorts, and worship a God and Goddess. The most amazing thing to me, however, was that they specifically state it makes no difference what a person's "creed, race, ethnicity, or sexual orientation is, the God and Goddess accept all their creations and love them equally." Hearing this made me feel better, and I continued to research all religions so I would have the upper hand when it came to questions I knew I would get. I again started to cast spells, which is a Wicca form of prayer. I loved the God and Goddess because they loved me and kept me from harm. Instead of feeling hatred and fear toward my divine creator, I felt love and happiness. I once again started to trust religion and slowly opened up to more people. With this newfound trust of religion I was able to fight people who still believe that gays should be persecuted for religious reasons. I am now a senior in high school and I have done many things to try and spread the message of love for all, no matter how they are different from each other. It has taken me a long time but I am no longer ashamed to be a homosexual, and I would not change that part of me for anything. While I still hear comments directed at others, and still feel the hatred and fear some people have, I am hopeful that it will all work out.

Finally, I am able to say that I believe it is possible for gay persons to be proud of themselves and their religion without fear of what God thinks of them. There are also those who realize some of the passages in the Bible are not to be taken literally. These are the people I hope will try to make a difference in a gay person's life. Homosexuals are being more accepted in today's society and I can only hope that the future will bring about more tolerance towards all people, no matter whom they love.

12

Janée

I began the coming-out process when I was nineteen years old. I went to a Christian high school and from there a Christian college. Both places provided atmospheres I knew I could not come out in. During my sophomore year of college I went to an off-campus program in San Francisco called Urban. While I was there, we studied one topic of oppression each month. We began with racism, then we studied sexism, and finally heterosexism. This was the first time I realized there were other interpretations of the classic "gay texts."

I was slowly coming out to myself during this whole semester. I was terrified. Most of the time I felt extremely evil and dirty. I prayed a lot, but I was pretty sure that God felt the same about me as the Church did. Many nights I could not sleep in my room alone because I was so scared. I felt as though my world was crumbling around me. I was going to lose my family. I was not talking to any of my friends about what was going on, and I felt hopeless about God and the Church. I felt completely alone, facing the scariest thing I could imagine.

It was during this time in the Urban program that I began to feel that organized religion was shallow and dogmatic. The students in the program represented a range of Christian beliefs from fundamental, inerrant views of the Bible to students whose only connection to Christianity was in their past. About halfway through the semester, I attended a Bible study open to both faculty and students that was led by one of the students. As we went around sharing prayer requests, it struck me that I was in an atmosphere where I could not ask for prayer, although I desperately needed it. Immediately after this, a faculty member asked someone to pray for a painful situation in his family. The girl who offered to pray for him said something like this, "We know everything works out for the good. We pray for these family members that they will stay faithful to you, God." I was so frustrated that I got up during the prayer and left. The faculty member had exposed his pain and the student prayed about how everything turns out for the best. This was the beginning of my questioning of the authenticity of organized religion.

From this point I started a painful journey of deconstructing views imposed on me since birth. I felt depressed, alone, and angry. I still was not sure if my homosexual orientation was something God could ever accept or that I could ever embrace. I figured it was something I was just stuck with.

I was raised in a Conservative Baptist church. Black-and-white views were the foundation of our religion. We never discussed things like sex or smoking because we all knew what were correct, moral choices. Before I ever came out to my family, I knew there would not be a place for me in the church. In fact, because of my parents' religious affiliation, I wondered if there would be a place for me in the family.

My remaining years at college have provided me with a place to slowly evolve spiritually. Initially, I only came out to my housemates. I hid that aspect of my identity from everyone else; this resulted in a level of shame inside of me. If I couldn't tell other people about my sexual orientation, somewhere inside of me I must have felt that it was not okay to have homosexual feelings. It was not until I began to break through the fear of speaking up about my sexual orientation that I could work through spiritual issues.

Since I have broken away from organized religion, I have looked more to books such as *The Feminine Face of God* and *God is a Verb* to shape my nonmainstream views of God and spirituality. I have focused more on right relationships with people and life-giving decisions as opposed to doctrines and creeds. I've drawn on the humanitarian aspects of the gospel, and Jesus' ministry of compassion instead of aspects dealing with the ethos of purity. From these morals and values, I realized I was limited in my spirituality because I was not being honest with people. I was upholding a homophobic silence, which was suffocating for me.

I knew something had to change for me on campus. A gay friend of mine, Justin, and I decided we should come out on campus and direct our efforts towards trying to foster dialogue. The topic of homosexuality was hardly dealt with on our Christian college campus. Only a couple of the churches in our city are Open and Affirming, and most everyone knew the Bible speaks out against homosexuality. Therefore, there was no point to really discuss the issue.

Justin and I arranged to hold our meeting and speak in one of the dorm basements. The week leading up to the discussion, posters were placed all over campus reading : "The Gay Debate. . . . Two students who have identified themselves as gay or lesbian share their stories." This was not exactly the type of publicity we had in mind. The night we made our presentation, we spoke to a packed basement of over two hundred students. We knew it was important to make ourselves real as opposed to homosexuality remaining a religious/political issue. We briefly shared some of our coming-out stories and spent the rest of the time fielding questions.

The overall feeling of this experience was positive, but Justin and I did not want the dialogue to die. We had the school newspaper write an article on the discussion. The newspaper article was also a relief because we wanted to assume that we were out to everyone on campus. We hated not knowing whom we were out to and who did not know. We later accepted an invitation to speak in a classroom. We shared our stories at a panel discussion on "How to Be Friends with a Gay Person." We organized a three-part series on various gay issues.

Although the series was meant to reach out to people on campus, it also provided us with a place to shed some of the layers of shame that can grow when one is silent in a conservative atmosphere. I have felt very free and more comfortable with myself since I have honestly identified myself to other people. Since we spoke out on campus, we have been invited to speak with elders at a local church on how they could create a more positive atmosphere in their church for gay people.

I feel as though I will never be comfortable in an organized religion setting again since I have come out. I have come to the conclusion that having an organized religion results in an invisible boundary that separates the people who are accepted in the church and those who are not. I will never allow myself to transcend to the inner circle again after having experienced what it is like to be excluded. The church I have attended, which has been fairly conservative in nature, causes people to be pretentious. It does not allow its members to be honest about their struggles for fear of being banished to the marginalized fringes of organized religion.

I will continue to find acceptance and love from my friends, which is very important to keeping my spiritual life alive. I feel God in peaceful moments and draw on my idea of humanistic values to guide my relationships with people. The religious world I used to live in has crumbled, but from it has emerged an idea of God and love that can withstand even coming out to the world.

13

Tesia

My name is Tesia Vurek. I am your basic Caucasian (Polish, German, Italian, and American). I was raised part of my life in Napa, California, and then moved to Marin County when I was in eighth grade because my mom was going to seminary. (I am now a "PK"—pastor's kid.) A couple of weeks ago I moved to Sonoma County to live with my wonderful girlfriend. I identify as a lesbian and have been out for a little over a year. I plan to finish college and go into the profession of my dreams . . . although I am not sure what that is yet. I have a passion for photography but I am also scared to try to make a living from my creativity.

About a year ago I chose to come out in church. I am a member of the United Church of Christ and my mother is the pastor at Fairfax Community Church. At the time I was just beginning to realize that my life was not going to be turned completely upside down by coming out; in fact, my life was being turned right side up!

My mom's best friend was giving the reflection (sermon) for the day and I knew that she was going to be talking about butterflies. Since I see butterflies as my primary connection to God, I decided that I should come and listen. I did not, however, expect to come and make an even deeper connection between butterflies and my own process of self-discovery. As Jill talked about the transformation of butterflies—from the caterpillar to

the chrysalis and then to the beautiful butterfly—I began to realize that my coming-out process was indeed very similar to
that cycle.

When I was first beginning to question my sexuality I had a
boyfriend, but I was simultaneously falling madly in love with
the most beautiful person I had ever seen—a woman. Since I
had no idea what was going on with me I stayed with my
boyfriend for another six or seven months, which I now refer to
as my cocoon stage. I was not myself; I was not connected to
God; I was totally in the dark and completely lost. I spent a lot
of time hating myself for putting me through that stage, but
now I realize that it was a necessary step in the process of becoming a beautiful butterfly!

Even after I broke up with my boyfriend and came to terms
with what was going on—I am a lesbian—I went through an
even worse time of immobilizing depression. This is when I was
totally convinced that my life would never be the same, I would
never get a date again, my friends would hate me—my life was
out of control. Slowly, as I began to connect with gay, lesbian,
bisexual, transgender, and questioning (g/l/b/t/q) youth online, I
began to realize that my life was not over. It was, in fact, just
beginning.

Through the help of my friends and family, and through my
belief in doing what feels right, I began to have pride. I joined a
youth group at Spectrum (g/l/b/t/q organization for Marin) so
that I could meet other g/l/b/t/q youth, and I started coming out
to everyone I knew. I began to open my wings and fly.

When I came out in church I was welcomed with warm em-
bracing hearts and arms. All the women (and a few of the men)
came up to me after the service and told me how brave and wonderful I am. The woman who brought flowers for the altar
wrapped them up in a moist paper towel and gave them to me,
telling me that I definitely deserved them. My heart was soaring!
I knew that our church was considered "open and affirming"
but I had never known any openly gay people to attend regularly, so I really did not know how everyone would react. I could

never have dreamed of such an open and affirming reaction.

Because my church has been so supportive of my coming-out process, I feel like my own connection to God has grown so much stronger. I still don't exactly understand who, or what, I think God is, but I know that I can't imagine my life without God in it. Also, because of the support from my congregation, I had the strength to continue in my coming-out process. Every time I hit a rut they were there to give me the push to keep going. My own family has been my greatest supporters, but my church community helped make the safety net complete.

My biggest struggle now is to find other individuals from the gay, lesbian, bisexual, and transgender community who believe in, and celebrate, God. Because of the vocal religious right, Christians have the reputation of being condemning and definitely not accepting, thus giving us a very bad name in the g/l/b/t/q community. My mom has been very helpful in trying to change this pattern by writing letters to the editor and participating in Spectrum events as "an accepting and loving clergy member," but it seems to be *very* slow progress.

I feel very lucky because I have been given the strength to be as out as I want to be. Many youth cannot be out because their families, friends, coworkers, or church cannot accept them for who they are. One of my greatest wishes is that people can understand that we are your children. We are no different from our heterosexual peers—we choose to follow our hearts and love.

14

Eric

I am a Jew with a not entirely unique distinction. I'm sure there are others like me out there, but in my twenty-four years I've never met one. I am a Jew born on December 25th. The most typical reaction when I share my birth date? "December 25th? You're a Christmas baby!" I can understand why people get so excited. For a lot of my friends, and even more strangers, Christmas is one of the most special days of the year. Any mention of it (barring the few hectic days immediately preceding the holiday and those exhausted few immediately following) causes an elated response. Since I was four years old, the conversation has run fairly typically:

"Well, yes, I'm born on December 25th, but I'm Jewish."

"Oh, you're kidding. That's a shame! I bet you get cheated on gifts!"

Naturally, as an eager-to-please child, I was reluctant to cause disappointment in others by sharing this detail about myself. As I got a little older, I learned to say, "Well, it's not a shame, it's just different for you. I'm proud of being Jewish!" My sadistic grandparents, who owned an arcade in a local shopping mall, thought it was funny to drag me to the lap of the poor guy dressed as Santa and torture him with this routine each year.

Eight days after birth, a male Jewish child is given a Hebrew name at his briss, or circumcision. When my parents told their Rabbi that my English name was Eric, he explained that there was no direct Hebrew translation for Eric, and offered them two choices. They chose Yisrael Avraham. As a child, I always liked my Hebrew name because it contained Yisrael, the Hebrew word for Israel. My seven-year-old brain constructed Israel as a magical place where all of history actually started and everyone was Jewish. This was the complete opposite of my school and my town—where almost no one was like my family.

My Jewish education ran alongside my traditional public school. I spent Sunday mornings and Tuesday and Thursday afternoons learning Hebrew or studying Judaica—all the while hearing about and looking forward to my bar mitzvah. My bar mitzvah is the day when I would become a man under Jewish tradition. In addition to the explicit lessons of the Alef-Bet, Torah verses, and holiday rituals, I also learned a few unspoken lessons that seemed to be just as important. After I became a man, my Judaica textbook told me, my next important life cycle event (some time in the future) would be marriage to a Jewish woman, followed by having our own children. My bar mitzvah service took place on a cold December day when I was in the eighth grade (several weeks before my actual birthday, of course, so our non-Jewish guests could attend). This event was both beautiful and nerve-wracking. I chanted my Torah portions, from the stories of Jacob and Joseph, and sang along with my kind teachers, the two rabbis and our cantor. Some of our older relatives expressed dismay at the cantor's guitar-playing, claiming it was not traditional. I imagine that even her very presence, as a woman leading us in prayer, was equally distressing to some of them. But in our Reform congregation, the cantor's presence, and the guitar that accompanied her beautiful voice, was one of the most beautiful, most important, and holiest traditions I knew.

At the reception immediately following, the photographer who immortalized my bar mitzvah was careful to follow those unspoken lessons of my Judaica texts. In time, I would go from one rite of passage to the next, the pictures seemed to predict. In my pink shirt and navy suit, I am immortalized dancing with Anne, dancing with Stephanie, dancing with Amy, dancing with twin sisters Carla and Mia, none of whom are Jewish but all of whom are female.

While I continued my formal Jewish education, socializing as Jewish teenagers took on an additional aspect. We began to plan and participate in events through our Jewish youth group, the B'nai B'rith Youth Organization. And once again, like the lessons and rituals that had marked my Jewish education so far, we all wore an invisible talit, or prayer shawl, of compulsory heterosexuality. My first and only girlfriend, Ellen, was my date to my very first and only Beau-Sweetheart dance, an annual BBYO event. For five months Ellen and I dated, visiting with each other's families, attending each other's proms, and going to our BBYO meetings together. As our relationship progressed, however, I began to understand that something about it felt wrong. Not evil or bad, but just wrong. Ellen asked me why it always seemed that I wanted to spend more time with a male friend than with her. We struggled with communication, with sexuality, with understanding, and ultimately ended our relationship soon after my junior prom.

Along with this same male friend, J.J. (who I began to suspect was gay), I started to consider the ways in which my feelings for other guys were different from my feelings for Ellen, for whom I felt a seemingly nonsexual but nonetheless genuine affection. By the end of the school year, I identified myself as bisexual, and admitted to J.J. that I felt attracted to him. Thankfully, the attraction was mutual, and we began a clandestine relationship just after our junior year of high school. I went away for the summer, and for the entire summer, J.J. and I wrote cards and letters to each other. Just before I left, I understood that I was gay, and we immortalized our new and exciting relationship with loving messages in each other's school yearbooks. Unlike my experience with Ellen, dating J.J., kissing him, and expressing emotions for him felt far more natural and right.

The day after I returned, my parents took me for a ride in the car. I knew something was up when my mom sat in the back and asked me to sit in the front with my dad. We drove to a parking lot across the street from my middle school, a place where, according to Mom and Dad, we could talk without being interrupted. In the painful minutes that followed, my parents asked me about my relationship with J.J. Our affectionate yearbook writings had revealed to my parents the relationship we were all too eager to hide. And so I began my senior year of high school arguing with my parents on an almost-daily basis. Looking back, I realize that my stubbornness played a role in our disagreements. But their unequivocal love was tempered slightly by their disgust, frustration, anger, and embarrassment. They ignored J.J., who had once been a welcome fixture in our home, and placed strong limitations on all of my social time.

With each day, my despair and frustration grew, as I felt increasingly angry at home, depressed in school, and sad at hiding so important a part of myself from my friends. My anger led me to what felt like a rational conclusion: there must be no God. Why would God create someone like me in her or his own image, and then distance me from my family and friends in a single stroke—especially one based in feelings about love? How could I be expected to believe in someone—or something—whose community of faith had made my very existence clearly unwelcome from childhood? So cruel a decision seemed unlikely of a compassionate God, and I began to doubt her or his existence more and more each day. One evening, the rabbi asked us to place ourselves somewhere on a line from point A to point B, representing our belief in God. Point A represented total, complete, and unequivocal faith, and point B represented no faith at all. Most students placed themselves somewhere in the middle. I carefully drew a chalk line just a centimeter away from point B. When the rabbi pressed me on this decision, I explained, "I am feeling hopeless, but I am not yet ready to give up."

I thought more and more about my connection to Judaism. What was it that made me Jewish? So many forces in my life made abandonment of Judaism seem logical. Because there were few Jews in my town, few of my friends were Jewish. Since coming out, I no longer felt welcome in my youth group. My public school, festively decorated for Christmas each December (supposedly mitigated by a "multicultural tree" in the front lobby), beckoned me to a non-Jewish existence. Even the date of my birth seemed to say, "You should be someone else." And so I began to explore.

I read, and I studied. I started back at the beginning, with my Hebrew name. Yisrael Avraham, they had chosen. I looked up the meanings of each name. Yisrael, the name given to Jacob when he wrestled with the angel of God. Yisrael—literally, he who strives with God. And Avraham—Abraham, the father of Isaac. I remembered a colorful tale in our childhood textbook of God testing Abraham on their covenant. Obeying Adonai's expectation of undying faith, Abraham nearly sacrificed his own son at God's command. Abraham—a man of undying faith. Yisrael—he who strives with God. Yisrael Avraham—he who strives with God but still has faith. That was me.

He who strives with God but still has faith. I believe, in my heart, that I have always been gay. I did not understand my sexual orientation and how it shapes the lens through which I see the world until I came out—until I named myself. And I know that I have always been Jewish, but I did not understand my faith and how it shapes the lens through which I see the world in the same exact way—until I named myself. Of course, self-acceptance is only the beginning of the process. Judaism, in my experience and in my belief, thrives when community thrives. It became even more important that I be a part of a community, that I learn with others and from others and, likewise, that I share my own experiences with others. I have found wonderful connections with other bisexual, gay, and lesbian Jews, and I have also returned to my home synagogue and other synagogues to find connections there.

More often than not, my community has surprised me. Yom Kippur can be a particularly painful day for lesbian, bisexual, and gay Jews. On this day, the verses from Leviticus so often cited as condemnation of homosexuality are among those read from the Torah. But my rabbi, my teacher, used one particular Yom Kippur as an opportunity to convey an important message to us. He shared his belief that bisexual, lesbian, and gay Jews should be welcomed as part of our community and that our unions should be recognized and blessed just as the unions of men and women. There is still a long way to go and there is still too much silence. Nevertheless, one or two of our synagogue's more prominent members and staff have begun to appear with their same-sex partners on important days—days to be shared with family. We are all beginning to be acknowledged as family—as a family who strives with God, but still has faith.

The lessons in the Torah, those which seem to deny my existence or my humanness, are there to challenge us. They are there to ask us to think about that which makes us human, and that which makes us whole. They are there to ask us to strengthen our faith by striving with God, by doubting and interpreting and learning and teaching. I was not raised to take every word of Torah literally; I was raised to ask questions and to learn from the lessons of my father and my mother and my father's fathers and my mother's mothers and all those who came before us. Intentionally or unintentionally, I was taught from childhood that to be a gay Jew was a contradiction. But like my name, it is not a contradiction. It is a revelation. Only through striving with God did I begin to understand my belief in God. And only through becoming a whole person—through beginning to understand my sexual orientation—did I begin to understand my faith.

15

Chad

If there is any one thing that has made my coming out as a gay man easy, it is, ironically, a church. The irony will be obvious to any observer of the current U.S. religious scene. Most churches are devoted to making it difficult, or at least inconvenient, to be gay. The Rev. Fred "God-hates-fags" Phelps is perhaps the most direct interpreter of the church's views. [Rev. Phelps, a minister from Texas, sponsors the website GOD-HATES-FAGS.com and organizes protests against g/l/b/t people.] Baptists, Presbyterians, Methodists, Catholics—none of these denominations really like queer folk any better, but they tend to be more discreet and politically correct. As far as that goes, most Episcopalians probably fall into the same category.

It was kind of an accident that we ended up at an Episcopal church. We first attended a little Methodist church on the corner. It was chosen because it was close to where we lived. Previously, we had been Methodist. But on that sticky summer Sunday, open windows provided the only ventilation in that Methodist church, and the attitude of the members seemed even less open than the windows. Years later, I still remember. No one said hello as we arrived or left. We got the message and didn't go back. I doubt if any other first-time visitors returned either. An African American Pentecostal congregation now occupies the building, and that corner really rocks now on Sunday nights.

By the time Q day, the day I knew for sure that I was gay, rolled around, our family had been at the Episcopal church most Sundays we were in town. Mom was there at least a couple of other times a week as well. The thing is, we were in church with quite a number of openly gay men—and some lesbians too. I, however, have never been able to easily identify them. Long before we knew them as gay or lesbian we knew them as Rick and his partner Sammy, Alice and her frequent visitor Sandy. Alberto, the maitre d' in the main restaurant of the hotel my dad managed, came to church on occasion, almost always accompanied by whichever of the many gay visitors in town that week had caught his eye.

Q day is etched in my memory. The memory is vivid not just because it became so clear to me, but also because I feared all the other guys in the locker room must have figured it out too. It was Matt's first year at this high school. His family moved to our city because of the Navy. Matt had stayed after school to try out for the junior varsity football team but had not thought about how he was going to get home afterward. As I started home on my little motorbike that afternoon, I saw Matt standing in the parking lot looking pretty forlorn. It was a long walk to the trailer park where Matt lived with his parents and younger sister. He was new to the island and probably could not have found his way home even if he had been willing to walk.

So, when I found out Matt's problem, it seemed the most natural thing in the world to do was to offer him a ride home on my cycle. I had no ulterior motive. Honest. Once we were on the way, I realized how delicious it was to have his strong arms around my shirtless torso. Matt had held on for his dear life. There was nothing between me and Matt's very strong arms, and I guess I should have known then that my goose bumps meant something. But I didn't figure it out at the time. Anyway, once Matt hopped off the bike and I headed home, I didn't think about him again until he smiled at me in homeroom the next morning. From that smile onward, we hung out together pretty much all the time. We were on the wrestling team together and roomed together when traveling off the island to meets. We went to movies and the beach together and were best friends as only a couple of fifteen-year-olds can be. By the time sophomore year was finished, my own mother was speculating that she probably saw more of Matt than his mother did. We were buds! Nothing all that unusual here; I know lots of straight guys who spent an inordinate amount of time hanging out with their best friend in tenth or eleventh grade.

Our family spent most of the summer after sophomore year away from town. Dad works for a big hotel company, and we traveled with him to a six-week training program and almost a month's vacation after that. Matt had spent the summer working and had already started pre-season football practice by the time I got back to town. We didn't reconnect until two nights before school started. Matt called up after getting home from football practice one afternoon to see if I was back, and immediately invited himself over to our place for a swim.

My mom and dad were out for the evening, so it was just Matt and me. We splashed around in the pool, cooked some burgers on the grill, and told each other stories of the summer. It was terrific getting acquainted again. Matt said he had been lonely most of the summer and told me he was really happy to have me back in town. I teased him about not having found a girlfriend over the summer, as a couple of our other friends had. Each of us had a sixteenth birthday coming within the next few weeks, and I said it seemed like we both would be "sweet sixteen but never been kissed." A couple of hours later, after we had watched a stupid movie on TV, Matt took off for home. On his way out the door, he quickly pulled my face toward him and kissed me on the cheek, saying, "Now you've been kissed!" I thought nothing of it. It was the sort of silly thing we did with each other.

The day before Q day, two things happened. Our health education teacher, Mr. Preston, announced that the following week we would take up the subject of homosexuality and that we should be thinking about any questions we had. One of the "brighter" members of our class waved his hand in the air and asked, "Mr. Preston, what's a hooo-moooo-sex-uuuuelll? Do you mean a 'queee-yer'?" Something about the way he asked it made me shiver, and I looked across the room at Matt, who rolled his eyes. The bell rang for lunch, and Mr. Preston wisely skipped trying to answer. He might have been trampled by hungry sixteen-year-olds making their way to the lunchroom.

After school that day, Matt told me he wanted to talk to me about something. Through the fall, Matt had been on the football team, so I hadn't seen much of him, and I had no idea what might be going on. So we went and sat under a tree at the beach while he told me his mother had been diagnosed with cancer and would almost certainly die before he graduated from high school. Because his father had been at sea so much during his early childhood, Matt and his mother were extremely close, and he had been hit hard by the news. I didn't know what to say except that I'd be praying for him and his mother. It was a dumb thing to say. My last prayer had been something I mumbled when the rector had dinner with us and for some reason he deflected onto me the request that he say grace. I did tell my mom about Matt's mother and how worried I was about him. She said, "You must care for him very much."

The day I knew for sure that I was gay was the first day of wrestling practice for the season. Since I hadn't played football in the fall like Matt and several of the other guys, I was pretty out of shape, and was behind almost everybody else heading for the shower. Towel slung casually around my neck, I noticed Matt ahead of me. I have no idea where this came from, but I yelled, "Hey, hot stuff." Two things happened simultaneously. Matt turned around, ready with some flip rejoinder. And my horny adolescent body reacted unmistakably to some combinations of my feelings for Matt, the sensations of a tough workout just completed, and the particular combination of curves and angles of my buddy's muscular form as he walked naked toward the shower. It's every guy's nightmare. An erection in a high school locker room is dangerous, and never more so than it was that day. "So now we know why you guys spend so much time together," was the kindest of the catcalls, and the only one I remember. My face flushed. I couldn't breathe. I didn't know what to say. I couldn't just ignore the teasing like I normally would because somehow I knew it was true. The occasional fantasies and dreams I'd had suddenly made sense. I wanted Matt sexually. Talk about coming out! I had just crashed out of a closet I didn't even know I was in.

I don't remember exactly what happened next. Somehow I managed to get showered, dressed, and on the way home in about three minutes without talking to anybody. An early supper was being put on the table when I arrived. My folks were headed for a meeting at church and didn't have time for the usual, "How was your day?" chat, which was just as well. An hour later, the phone rang. It was Matt.

"You sure did take off in a hurry after practice," he said. "Anything wrong?" He was acting like nothing had happened. I couldn't believe it!

"Well duh," I told him. "What do you think?"

"Oh that. It could happen to anyone. Don't worry about it. Besides, you are kinda cute when you blush."

If Matt had been in the same room with me, I wouldn't have known whether to smash his face in because he was taking so lightly something that had freaked me out or to hug him because he was making it easy for me. We could just forget anything had happened. I replied, "If you keep saying I'm 'kinda cute,' the guys are gonna think we're fags for sure!"

Matt spoke into the phone more quietly, an unusual thickness in his voice. "Chad, you are cute. And I think we might be feeling the same way about each other."

I will never know where Matt got the courage to tell me that. It may well be the most important gift he could ever give me. Matt says he didn't really think much about it in advance, and he didn't think it much of a risk. It came spontaneously, the way people's most honest statements often do. Hearing his words, I was hugely relieved. Riding home from school that evening, my biggest fear had been that I would lose my friend. Instead it looked like the event might bring us closer. But, honestly, I was scared. I didn't know what to say.

Matt's voice on the phone brought me back. "Chad, are you there? What are you thinking?"

"Matt, thanks for calling. I'm confused right now. I don't know about you but I am just figuring out what some of my thoughts and feelings have meant. What do you think it will be like at school tomorrow?"

He said not to worry about it, that if I hadn't left in such a hurry I would have heard my big-mouthed teammates asking whether I really had the idea they thought I was queer. They had just been teasing me about a physical manifestation they all worried about constantly. It seemed my cover was safe. I understand now that this is a kind of privilege you have if you don't fit the stereotypical image of a "fag." At six foot, three inches and 200 pounds, with a deep voice and no "swish" in my walk, I could pass as straight, as long as nobody told the guys how much I liked to watch ballet or ice skating!

"Let's get together after practice tomorrow," I suggested. "We'll talk more then. I'm exhausted."

I was exhausted because my mind had been working furiously since fleeing the locker room. I had overreacted, and I knew it even before Matt told me. At any other time, I might have bluffed my way through the teasing by swaggering around salaciously until everybody else got embarrassed, or bored, and left me alone. But that day I was vulnerable because what my mind had undoubtedly been working on for months had finally come to the conscious level.

My family had been living in this tourist town for almost five years at that point, and the island had been a popular gay tourist destination for many years before that. A person walking or driving through downtown would have to be in a coma not to notice the many obviously gay men on the sidewalks, in the shops, and enjoying the restaurants and bars that open onto the street. By "obviously gay," I mean the handsome, carefully dressed, athletically trained men that quickly activate what I now call my "gaydar." Through acquaintances at church, I learned many others, not so obvious, are also part of our gay family. Even before meeting Matt, I had sensed that I had something in common with many of those men. At first, I thought it was just the attention I paid to my appearance. But when I would occasionally meet the eye of someone I found attractive, I knew there was more.

In my earliest teen years, my sexual dreams and fantasies had been somewhat vague, but they almost never involved women. After the first time Matt rode behind me on the motorbike with his strong arms clasped tightly around my bare torso, those fantasies began to be much more specific. For some reason, I had not put a label on myself until that afternoon in the locker room. It took a while, I think, because without knowing it, I had internalized so many messages that being gay was a bad thing. I had always resisted being categorized, and with the well-known human capacity for denial added, it became much easier to understand my denial.

So why was I so freaked out about being gay? In my case, it was certainly not that my parents or anyone else specifically made a point about it being bad. It was more like something polluting the water or the air. Long before they know what it means, kids learn that calling someone a "fag" is the ultimate insult. And of course, there is the fact that people are generally assumed to be straight. The absence of visible gay people as admirable characters in fiction or nonfiction literature, film, and television, sends a very strong message about being gay. I don't remember anyone ever mentioning gay people in church before we moved, so there had been no particular negative message there either. Rev. Phelps had not yet begun to travel around the country picketing gay pride demonstrations and funerals with his hate-filled epithets. On the other hand, I would never have known from my early days in church that gay and lesbian people even existed, let alone that they could be good members of a community. I remember admonitions against racism, which the pastor referred to as discrimination, but none against gay bashing. Nevertheless, it did not occur to me to conceal my gay identity from my parents, once I knew for sure. I took some time to figure out what, when, and how to tell them. I did tell them at dinner a few nights later. Dad laughed when I described the locker room scene, but one look from Mom shut him up. They had just two concerns: my risk of getting AIDS, and the probability that my happiness would be limited by the bigotry that still exists in society.

Matt and I found out about the latter very quickly. In school the day after Q day, it was like nothing had happened. During the evening after supper, Matt and I met on the beach to talk about what was happening to us. We built a small (and illegal) fire and talked quietly for a couple of hours. We were sitting with our arms around each other, enjoying first kisses, when two or three men came up behind us and started to yell. Because we had been looking into the fire, we couldn't see them when we turned around, but they immediately started throwing sand in our faces, calling us every nasty name for homosexuals I'd ever heard, and threatening to teach us "what being a fag is really like." At first I was scared, but then I got angry. And when I got angry, I remembered that Matt and I knew how to take care of ourselves pretty well—as long as they did not have weapons. So we stood up and faced them. Matt is not as tall as I am, but he weighs about the same. His tank top and gym shorts left little about his strength to our attackers' imagination, and they knocked each other down trying to get away.

There is a lot of physical violence against gay people, probably much more than can be monitored accurately. Many people don't bother to report an assault, assuming correctly in most cases that the cops won't do much about it. Others are afraid of having their sexuality exposed. But once I began to pay attention to what is going on with gay people in society, I concluded that the churches are a much more significant threat to us. There are a few exceptions; however, the church attacks us emotionally through mixed messages like, "Hate the sin and love the sinner," or "Don't be promiscuous, but we won't bless your relationships." Many actively oppose civil rights protections and laws against hate crimes. Our best hope may well be that churches' influence will continue to decline. Unfortunately, those church people whose faith motivates them toward affirmation of difference and active service to disadvantaged people seem drastically outnumbered. Their voices are definitely drowned out by those whose actions and messages are innocuous at best and hateful at worst. The ancients evaluated the power of competing gods by the potency and value of their influence in the world. Judged on that basis, the disappearance of Christianity would be at worst a neutral change.

As far as I can tell, the problem is not really what is stated in the Bible. There are those dozen or so passages that use words like "abomination" to refer to us. But reading the Bible like that, you can also say the Bible promotes slavery and forbids us to enjoy lobster. The real problem seems to be that people use the Bible to justify their feelings of hatred and prejudice against us. What is most troubling is how little you see of the church as an opponent to those attitudes and the behaviors that flow from it.

Matt and I are trying to build a relationship that makes sense. His mother died a week after high school graduation. Because his father has not been able to accept Matt's gayness or our relationship, losing his mother was like losing his family. My parents do what they can to fill the void. My parents' ability and willingness to support nightly telephone conversations and frequent visits have made it possible for us to move beyond the early adolescent crush we discovered so suddenly, despite going to college a thousand miles apart. It might be trite to say it, but our love for each other is deep. We recognized it would be silly for a couple of horny college guys to promise sexual exclusivity to each other. Instead, we have made honesty and a relentless avoidance of jealousy as the mainstays of our relationship. We are also clear that each of us is the other's main man. We expect to begin building our lives together in a new way when we finish college. We plan to live in San Francisco, where my first-choice medical school is located.

I want us to incorporate a spiritual component into our life together, and I wish we could have a community of people like the ones I got to know at church in high school. But I cannot participate in an institution like the Christian church that seems so tolerant of hatred against gay people. The way Matt says it is this: "Remember they count the people in church every Sunday, and I don't want to be included in that count."

Beyond the churches' institutional failings, the idea of a supernatural god seems very unreal to me. The one thing I have internalized from my childhood and teenage religious experiences is a powerful sense of connectedness with other people and with the world, indeed with the universe. We have begun to find a few people we are thinking of as our chosen family. Some are gay, some are not. What is important about these friends is that they honor and support the love Matt and I have been finding with each other, just as we treasure their closest relationships. In these connections we find compassion, hope, and even courage. Isn't that what faith is really about?

16

Jeffrey

This is an abbreviated script of an interview with Jeffrey, a female-to-male transsexual who is the founder of a support group for transgender youth.

Does your family support you in your gender identification? If so, how has this helped you?

Yes, my family is very supportive of my life. As my family and I are transitioning into my male gender identity, presentation, and sexuality, we have become closer emotionally. Though I am living independent from my family of origin, my father and mother accept me. They only want me to be happy, healthy, and productive. My family does not financially help me pay for medical and mental health care, yet because I was under the legal age of consent when I made my gender change, they were involved with the decision-making process. I am lucky in that my parents are college educated and I had access to affordable, appropriate health care.

Did you always feel confident to be open about gender-related issues with your parents?

My mother dressed me in pink, made me get my ears pierced when I was five, signed me up for ballet class when I was four. Until I moved out to college, she encouraged me to wear dresses and skirts, to pluck my eyebrows, to apply makeup, and to date boys. However, despite my mother's nagging, I was independent of her ways. Overall she and my father always encouraged individuality and self-identity. In addition, sexuality was not taboo in my household, and I've learned about safe sex, pregnancy prevention, homosexuality, and transexuality since I was five.

How have they accepted you?

During my coming out to my father, he became very angry. He then kicked me out of his apartment and I was homeless. That fight with my Dad catalyzed my move to complete financial independence from my family of origin, and also was my first taste of rejection by those I love. I was eighteen. I had to geographically relocate in order to discover my own self. I think that they have learned to do the same with the choices I make. Right now, my mother has accepted my male identity, but she is feeling a loss of me as her daughter rather than the gain of me as her son. I have a younger brother too. My Dad has respected the boundaries of my adulthood, and he is trying to accept my body as it is physically growing up. Dad understands on an intellectual and personal level the changes that my body is experiencing, yet he is throwing moralistic philosophical crap about the sex change in my face. He has not accepted the medical necessity of sex reassignment surgeries. He is scared for both my mental state of mind and my overall health. I assure him that I am seeing the most trained gender specialists, a team of health care professionals that includes an endocrinologist, a general practitioner, a team of clinical psychologists, and a plastic surgeon. I also attend a monthly support and social group for people who self-identify along the FTM (female-to-male) continuum. As a result of my parents' initial lack of support, I had to advocate for my own needs; I had to learn to ask for what I want and what I need.

How do you feel about pop culture's lack of information about transgender people?

Any time a new idea is introduced into a given society, it must be filtered through the eyes of the mainstream/dominant culture. Transgenderism is not an idea. It is not a concept. It is not a trendy academic class. We are not a disease, nor groups of people to be studied like gorillas in the mist. We are not homosexuals in denial nor freaks of nature. We are not entertainment. Simply put, people who are transgender are people, like you and me. To have a transgender identity is to claim a nonconformist gender presentation, identity, and/or expression that is incongruent to the dominant/mainstream/pop culture's definitions of socially acceptable ways of being. Therefore, within the context of pop culture, the transgender experience is often misrepresented in the media, stigmatized by the queer community, pathologized by the medical institution, demonized by communities of faith, and targeted for the most violent of hate crimes throughout the world. Transgender identities cross all cultures, all spiritual denominations, all economic levels, all categories of race. We have able bodies and differently abled bodies, encompass all political affiliations, all sexual orientations. Transphobia, or the conscious ignorance of people whose sex, sexuality, and/or gender do not conform to pop culture, is why one transperson dies every month.

Do you feel that you were born knowing you were male or did experiences in your life convince you that you were a different gender?

Gender is different from sex. My gender has always been "traditionally" male. However, being a gay male in our society means that I do not conform to the traditional male role. That is something I do not understand, however. To me, there is nothing more "male" than men having sex with men. So, the innate core of my being, that true sense of self, is male. As a male, I value and express my sensitivity, femininity, and fierce fashion sense. In this society, it is devalued for a male to experience being light in the loafers. Why? It's a power game. So, until women gain equal access, equal respect, and economic suffrage in our culture, effeminate men, gay men, femme lesbians, transgender women, transmen, transfags, and intersexed people will be "differently gendered."

*If you were the member of a different culture and time
period setting, do you believe you would identify yourself as
transgender?*

Yes. I was born with one body, brain, and spirit. The time is just right. Had I been born biologically male, I have no doubt that I would still be transgender. Most likely my body and mind would still have been sexed unbalanced to my one true universal spirit. Hence, crossing all time and cultures, I will always be transgendered.

Did you ever suffer from abuse as a result of your gender?

Yes. Most often I am verbally assaulted and harassed by clumps of teenage boys. I'm lucky, in a way, that I pass well in most social scenes as a "straight white male." While I know that passing gives me certain social privileges that I did not ask for, I also know that it protects me in some ways. However, when I am "read" as a gay man or as a transperson, I am the target for physical violence. In December of 1999 three teens of color repeatedly called me "fag" while on the public bus. As the bus pulled away from the curb of their stop, they threw a brick through the window of my seat. At other times I have been followed home, laughed at, stared at. People will literally move their seat on the Red Line, cross the street, cover their children's eyes. It's humiliating and dangerous to live in a state of androgyny, let alone femininity.

Have you felt discriminated against as a result of your gender?

Ironically, the most discrimination I face is within the gay and lesbian community. Should I be allowed to go to the men's-only discussion group? Sure, if I pass well enough. Should I be allowed to go to the Cambridge Women's Center? Sure, because I'm not a "real" man. Screw that! I don't want to be at either one of those places then.

*What kind of neighborhood did you grow up in (urban,
suburban, country, etc.)?*

I grew up in a cookie-cutter straight, white, middle-class suburb of Connecticut. Yet, my parents made sure that I was raised with freedom, without prejudice, and with high moral standards. My dad was the Sunday school superintendent, and my mother is a high school special education teacher. I have always placed little value on money, and more on the importance of people. I attended a regional public high school, held a job for three years in a family-owned restaurant, and helped care for my mom, as she has many physical limitations.

What is your sexual orientation?

I'm half gay and I'm half straight. There is nothing really to figure out. I think that people are so concerned with how bodies match up, like how 1+1=2, or that boy+girl=sex, that people really limit love. I am attracted to nice people and nice people are attracted to me. I am a boy bottom and I have sex with men. The way I see it, lesbian, gay, or bisexual is how one body relates to another body. Right now, I am just beginning to relate to my own body, to come into my own self. In a nutshell, that is the difference between sexuality, sex, and gender identity.

Did you always think you were born the wrong gender?

I knew that I had no future living to be what society expects female-bodied people to be.

Do you think there is an event from your childhood that caused you to feel like the wrong gender as you were growing up?

Looking back, there are many scenes, events, people, and situations I remember in which I felt different. However, there was no difference between me and the other boys in school until about middle school. That's when the other boys had their groups and the girls had their cliques. I was never part of any of that teen development. I get to experience all that and round two of acne now!

In what ways do you conform to your gender role?

I'll describe myself to you. Based on whatever definitions you have about gendered roles, you can decide in what ways I fit your definition of male and in what ways I am not "traditional." Physically, I wear my hair buzzed close to the scalp and a little longer on the top. My sideburns (when I have them) and my back hairline are squared rather than pointed. I clip my fingernails to the edge. I wear jeans, Timberland work boots, and flannel shirts. I also wear pants, suits, button-down oxfords that button on the left, and conservative neckties. I play basketball and lift weights. I am five foot three inches on good days, weigh 130 pounds, and have really small hands. I wear a leather jacket. I talk assertively, stand up on the T, and give my seat up to old ladies. Girls ask me out, I woo with flowers and dinner and trips. I play all day long on the computer, I carry my wallet in my back pocket rather than the front, and I don't wear a watch or glasses. I don't have any facial hair, my voice is rather soprano, I am caring, warm-hearted, and love to take peach bubble baths. I am artistic, love to shop for furniture, kitchenware, and athletic clothes. I date boys and girls. I hope to someday get married and raise a family in the suburbs. I would also like to travel, become an ordained minister, and be the founder and investor of a transcultural center. Asked once during an exercise at a conference to stand up if I identified as any of the labels mentioned by the facilitator, I stood at the following terms: FTM, transman, male, transgender warrior. Asked to say any other identity we claimed if it had not been mentioned, I proudly responded, "Jeffrey!" That's who I am.

17

Heather

When I was a young child, my grandparents would take my twin sister and me to Catholic mass. The priest would talk about life, death, heaven, gays, and war-things you don't think about when you are younger. To tell you the truth, I never knew what being gay was until I was old enough to realize what my feelings were telling me. I remember being told that gays were bad.

My sister and I excelled in sports. By the time we were in high school we had already made the varsity team in softball. While in my sophomore year I hurt my knee and ended my athletic career. I had no idea it would change my life so much. I ended up on crutches for two years and had given up on myself and on God. By that spring I was in a wheelchair. I went through twenty-three procedures, and finally I realized at the age of eighteen that I had a permanent disability. I was going to be in constant pain for the rest of my life. I was so angry with God for doing this to me. I thought God was there to protect me; how could God do this to me? I had been there for so many other people, giving my life to help others, and this is how God repays me? At the peak of all this, my mom and dad tried to get us back into the church but I was so angry at God that I could not see past the pain and the hurt.

I worked through the physical therapy and the pain to get walking on my own two feet, and as I look back I don't know how I did it all on my own. I realize now that I didn't. I have been through more in my twenty-one years on this earth than most people will have to go through in their lifetime. I now know that through all the lonely nights and painful days, God is there to give me the strength to make it through.

I am still haunted with memories of coming out in high school. I remember all of the teasing, jokes, name calling, and death threats directed at both my twin sister and me. I kept thinking that if something bad was to happen, I couldn't run like my sister. I was stuck in a wheelchair and there was nowhere for me to go. For that reason, I tried to keep my relationship with my lover a secret so she could possibly live a "normal" life. Now, three years later, I am still afraid to show my true love for her away from the confined walls of our home.

I am now in a relationship with a remarkable woman. I want to spend the rest of my life with her. I know now that God will accept everyone! I can finally say that I am starting to find the love for myself and the people around me—now that I realize that it's God getting me through life.

18

Matthew

I am walking up and down a path of light and darkness. There are faces I see staring at me. Some faces shine love and acceptance and others do not want to even look me in the eye. Different words spoken all confuse me, comfort me, and hurt me. Today my path is brighter as I move closer and closer into the light. Let me tell my story and where it began in that dark place of despair. I have been continually reaching and reaching into the light. I've almost found it.

It was a cold winter morning during twelfth grade and I was sitting in English class trying to learn something amid my raging hormones. I rolled up the sleeves of my heavy shirt as my eyes began to wander around the room. I came to realize something this very day that would change my life forever. My eyes seemed to stop when I came to two individuals who were sitting together sharing a textbook. Although Lauren looked attractive in her sweater and dress, there was something about Jeremy that really caught my eye. Was it his bright blue eyes or his broad shoulders that made me so attracted to him, or was it the way he smiled or his warm personality? I was feeling something that was leading me into forbidden territory. This was not the first time I had looked at other guys and found them desirable, but this was the first time that I began to understand and know that the feelings I had were strong and needed to be addressed.

During my senior year of high school I began to stop denying my sexual orientation and let go of my secret for the very first time. At times I did not know what to do or whom I could talk to. I did not even know if I was gay; maybe I was just confused. Maybe I just needed to experiment a little. Was I lacking a significant relationship in my life, since everyone else around me seemed to have a boyfriend or girlfriend? While interviewing my high school counselor for a story on troubled youth, the words slipped out of my mouth at long last. My hands were shaking as I told her what was so deep within my soul and that it had taken everything for me to seek her knowledge and guidance that day. I know God was with me in the office and encouraging me to seek the truth through understanding myself better. I told her I thought I might be gay, but I think I knew in my heart what the truth really was. The word gay was used as a weapon against me for years and so I related it to something sinful and awful. In turn, I needed to find a way out of the mess I was creating for myself. Could I be changed? I asked my spiritual nurturer to help me. I really needed help from anyone who could offer it. Down the road I would understand what it meant to be a gay man, but this of course would take time, energy, and endless struggles. I certainly was physically and emotionally attracted to the same sex, more than I was to women. This is all I knew.

The counselor was the first person who told me it was okay to have these feelings. It was okay to be gay. How refreshing and reassuring those words were to hear. What I was feeling inside myself wasn't unusual, sinful, or awful. There had to be so many others out there just like me. I was determined to find them. I would come out to my parents and friends, and continually come out over the next two years. There would be broken relationships and new ones formed. I would try to change my sexuality to conform to standards all around me, but it would not become a reality. It is these struggles that have made me more secure in who I am.

One night in 1997 my mother asked me why I was not doing well in school and why I seemed so distracted. I was so frustrated by my parents' inability to understand me and I thought it was about time to tell them what was on my mind. I did not expect a warm welcome from my mother after I told her I was gay, but I had to be honest and truthful no matter what the consequence. After the words slipped out of my mouth she ran upstairs and told my father, who was sleeping, that her son was gay. The bomb had hit. Over the next few days every picture of me came off the wall and I was called every name in the book. I was told that what I said couldn't be true. I didn't walk like a girl, have earrings, or talk in a feminine way. Being gay was all about wild sex and partying. My parents' reaction was probably expected but it proved to me that love can be very conditional.

Things eventually quieted down and we went back to pretending that I was straight. I am an only child and all of the expectations have fallen upon me. Must I be everything they want me to be? Yes, I want to please my parents and make them proud. I want our relationship to be the same as it was before I told them I was gay. Two years later they still do not talk about it and continue to threaten me with what will happen if I truly am gay. I know my parents love me and that one day they will understand what I have been feeling all these years. Life is fragile and short and I need to do what makes me happy, and they will see in time that loving another human being is not all bad. There may even be grandchildren! I hope God can help them know that their son is the same as he always was—a loving, compassionate, and truthful individual who desires the same from others.

It is very difficult to form intimate relationships when parents disapprove. The sneaking around, the quiet conversations, and the feelings of guilt do not help to build healthy relationships. I have found that having different types of relationships can be both helpful and harmful. The only connection I had to the gay community at the time I graduated from high school was on the Internet. I found people I could talk to and relate to in a safe environment without giving away any personal information. It was wonderful to be talking and sharing with others who were feeling like I was. I was only beginning to experience this new phase in my life.

We all expect different things from our partners and my first relationship was based more on experimentation than substance. It is hard to see the faults in people who seem so right, but are so wrong. As I have continued on my journey, I have found what I do like and what I do not like. It is the experience of meeting different people, getting hurt, and knowing what that feels like that has made me realize what I am truly looking for—a committed, loving relationship without the expectations of something that will never be. I deserve to be loved fully.

I thought there was no way that the church could be a source of support, but what I thought was wrong. I now know that God has been following me on this journey since day one. Although not visible at first, the church and my faith in God has played a huge role in moving me into the light. As a lifelong member of the United Church of Christ, I have been active at both local and national levels. Maybe God knew that I would need this source of support in the years to come. I thank those within the church who have made such a difference in my life.

My home church is friendly but not welcoming. I believe that if most people knew the real me I would not have the same relationship with the church. I was able to talk about my sexuality with my church pastor and the difficulties I was having with college while home on spring break in 1998. Never in my life did I think that I would hear loving and compassionate words about being gay coming from my church pastor. In my journey, I view this as a crossroads because the church and my inner being became reconnected at this point. I knew I was a child of God no matter whom I loved and that left me feeling content. Being gay has recently affected my home church involvement due to my feelings of becoming more comfortable with who I am. I feel like I am hiding something at times and would like to open up, but it is very difficult depending on the leadership in the church at the time.

The pastor whom I felt so comfortable with is now gone and replaced with someone I cannot relate to. Even pastors who are comfortable with gay issues face extreme opposition from their congregations. I have found other churches that are open and accepting to anyone regardless of their sexual orientation. The spirit of God certainly fills these churches and that is probably where I will end up one day feeling most comfortable. Faith communities need to be portraying one clear message—that God's love is unconditional. It doesn't matter what you wear to church or whom you love in this life. The baggage needs to go. My image of God used to be rooted in fear and condemnation, but now it is one of salvation, understanding, blessings, and love. Our churches need resources, guidance, and stability to serve those in need. Change and the end of homophobia will only happen through education and positive examples.

I want people to know that it is very important for others to be helpful and supportive of g/l/b/t and questioning youth and young adults. I was lucky enough to have support within the church, with my friends, and in school. Not everyone is this fortunate. What I needed most were people I could open up to and share with. Everyone has a different story and a way of dealing with the decision to come out. Coming out is an ongoing process and in some situations we can't come out. There is much diversity in the gay community and it is easy to get confused by those we talk to, what we read, or where we live. It is important to get accurate and helpful information that does not confuse, mislead, or condemn.

My spiritual journey and faith in God have been strengthened through all of my struggles. I feel the joy and love of God in the person that I am today. I plan to be a teacher one day and want to help others understand that it is okay to be the person that God intended, no matter what others say. I am just me and that is all I can say. There is no mold I need to fit. God has blessed me with a gift, the ability to love another man in a way I never thought possible. Thanks be to God for the power of love and its ability to change lives. I continue to reach higher and higher for the light.

19

Bobbi

As a teenager, I remember not really feeling like I belonged at church. But my parents expected me to be there, and so I was, every Sunday, and at every youth group function, Sunday school, vacation Bible school, and children's choir. I suppose some people thought those activities really meant something to me. They didn't.

In high school, my athletic teams frequently practiced on Sunday afternoons and so I would show up in sweats and sneak out early to get to the gym. I was more comfortable in sweats and a t-shirt than frilly stuff anyway.

In college, suddenly going to church was something that was my choice. I went. When I began to interact with that group of students, I realized that I had a lot in common with them. A small group of us became very, very close. Gender was irrelevant (or so it seemed to me); we were all just wonderful friends.

Even though my church friends were important to me, there was still a large part of me that felt I didn't quite fit in. They were somehow better than I was. Trying in desperation to find some meaning in my life, I turned to alcohol and a whole new crowd. I could be happy and funny there, and it made meeting people easier. Too easy sometimes.

Let me step back for just a moment and include a little more background. I grew up in a small town in Ohio. When I left for college, I didn't even know any openly gay or lesbian individuals. Through high school and the first couple years of college I had dated occasionally—but looking back I realize that they were guys with no real potential of meaning anything to me. So when I first realized my feelings for one of those close female church friends, it didn't really surprise me. But I didn't feel like I could approach something like that with her. Instead, I expressed interest in one of my drinking buddies, and because of the alcohol, we found an opportunity to explore what we were feeling. Then I was sure about myself. To my dismay though, my friend was then sure she was not interested. But I found something special that I had never felt prior to that evening; I discovered the ability to emotionally and physically connect with another individual on a really meaningful level.

The next morning, I left for a retreat with my church friends. I couldn't keep the new free, happy feelings that were in my heart to myself. I knew it would be strange to tell my best female friends, so I asked one of the guys if we could talk for a minute. Alone, I told him what had happened the night before. He didn't seem surprised at all. I also told him that I didn't want to give up hope of kids, and a "real" family and so I thought I was bisexual. I think we both knew the truth then, but I wasn't ready to accept it.

Within a few days, my other friends were suspecting something was wrong because I was being a little distant with them. So I ended up telling a couple more close friends, including the one I had feelings for, but I didn't tell her that yet. Every one of them was very supportive! For the first time in my life, I really felt whole and loveable. Now I just needed to find someone to love me back.

My faith changed dramatically when I began to accept my sexuality. I did feel loveable, and that included by God. God didn't seem so distant and unapproachable anymore. I was also very lucky to have a wonderfully accepting campus minister, who encouraged my newfound happiness and my continued growth in faith. Like a disciple I would be persecuted for my views that differed from society, but my faith that God created me as a lesbian sustains the difficult times.

By graduation, my love interest and I had realized our feelings were mutual. Now we've been together almost a year. Even though there have been rough spots for both of us, and with our families, we are incredibly happy and content. I even eventually accepted the truth, there is no "normal" relationship in my future according to society's definition. But the relationship that I have is what is normal for me.

I had faced nothing but acceptance from the people that I had come out to on campus. Granted, those friends were carefully selected, but it was reassuring to know that so many special people in my life were supporting me. The trouble didn't arise until the summer. Back in my hometown, I was invited to teach a vacation Bible school (VBS) class, and had became quite involved with the preparations. One evening at a planning meeting, some of the other women involved realized I was upset about something. Eventually, I told two of them the truth. My girlfriend had called me that day to let me know that we were facing significant opposition from her parents. I was planning to move in with her in a month, and they were trying to prevent us from even seeing one another. I was completely blamed for "corrupting" their daughter.

That night those women were wonderfully helpful. They tried to support me, but also to help me to see how that would be a surprise and challenge for my girlfriend's parents. They also asked me how my parents were handling the news. This was ironic in itself because I had told my parents at about 5:30 in the morning, three days earlier, while they were loading the van to go on vacation. My rationalization was that it would give them time to process and discuss between themselves, before reacting. I think it worked. But it also gave me a week to stress about what they really were thinking and saying eight hours away. For strength, I had the fact that they took the news pretty nonchalantly. I think they had suspected I was a lesbian for some time but never quite knew if they should ask.

Anyway, those two women were wonderful that night, but it didn't take long to find out how they really felt. Both soon became distant, and made it clear that they were uncomfortable with me being around their kids. That week of VBS became very challenging. On Friday, I was supposed to teach this group of fourth to seventh graders that God loves everyone—even though I knew that some of their parents didn't even necessarily believe that God loved me. The kids were discussing types of people who are discriminated against, but whom God loves—mostly it was just people different from themselves: "black people, poor people, stupid people." Their list went on and on. They never mentioned gays and lesbians, and I knew that I couldn't be the one to bring it up, especially after the reactions of those women. And so I sat, quietly disappointed, and then changed the topic.

At the end of the summer, I moved across the state for graduate school and quickly found a Reconciling Congregation full of wonderful, loving, compassionate people. These people loved me for me and didn't care whom I loved. I felt like I had known them forever, after only a couple of weeks.

I was asked by another local pastor if I would speak to a Sunday school class at his church about my experiences related to my faith and my sexuality. I eagerly agreed. The first week I spent the whole time telling my story, mostly on my own—but with a few prompts of direction from their questions. The second week was an opportunity for them to speak up and react, and for me to field more questions. The first week I thought they were listening. The second week I realized they were still convinced I was wrong. They couldn't understand why it was important to me to go to a Reconciled church. I said my relationship wasn't something I was ashamed of, and I didn't want that to affect the way people viewed me as a person. Therefore I chose to surround myself whenever possible with people for whom my sexuality was not an issue. I tried to help them to see that to me my relationship was no different than each of their straight relationships—only the rest of society saw a difference.

Only the rest of society might react harshly if we walked through the mall holding hands, or lived together, or raised a family together. To us this is a normal relationship, and a normal life.

It was incredibly disheartening to see how little I affected their views. Not that I thought I could change them, but at least that they could respect me for me. Then the class ended. As I headed for the parking lot a man followed me and, with tears in his eyes, thanked me for coming. His stepson had recently come out to him and his wife—and they were really struggling with it. He was encouraged by hearing how "well adjusted" I seemed. He hoped that his wife (who was also in the class) had been really listening as well. Suddenly all the pain of the questions and the defeat that I felt were gone. I knew that I had at least impacted that one family—and maybe made the difficulty of dealing with someone's coming out a little easier for them.

Since moving here, a lot has happened in my life. For the first time, I am completely responsible for myself—financially, emotionally, etc. The only area of my life where I am particularly closeted is with the family of the student that I tutor. Luckily my girlfriend and I both have somewhat gender neutral names and so I can say that I spent time with her by name (and simply leave out pronouns) and never actually lie. In my heart I don't want to lie to them, but I also don't think that they would be very accepting, and so I continue. Additionally, I came to realize that my bad habits were hurting not only myself, but my relationship. And so I have not had any alcohol or cigarettes in several months. Yes, my girlfriend is very proud of me—but it's more than that. I'm proud of myself.

Prior to coming out, I didn't have a very powerful, personal image of God. Now God has a special place in my life, my heart, and my relationship. I know that God loves me. I feel like God has given me an opportunity to share the fact that I'm gay and I'm okay with others. I want to find ways to end the hatred, fear, and homophobia in our society.

20

Nathan

It has been two years since that day on the beach, when I thought I had seen the most beautiful being alive. It was also the first day I had officially come out to myself. It was amazing. I finally had a true sense of who I really was after years of soul searching. The first thought that came to my mind was not, "Will God still love me?" Because I already knew that answer.

I have always been a very religious person. It was a way of filling up the hole of unfulfillment that I had when I didn't know I was gay. I have been everything. The first thing I experimented with was a Pentecostal Baptist church down the road from where I was currently living. I then moved onto Catholicism and into Buddhism. But that was still not enough. I practiced Hinduism, Taoism, and finally Jehovah's Witness.

But the religion that has really helped me through all the tumult I have experienced is the ever-growing Wicca. It was a way for me to balance my intellect and spirit and become a better person. With Wicca, every day brought new things and my life was filled with the magic and mystery of the unknown. It not only accepted gay people, but worshipped them as spiritual leaders and healers. Finally, a religion that could acccept me.

Over the time I experimented with these religions, I came out to my friends, immediate family, and God. Something was missing, though, and I didn't know what. Day after day I came home and cried until my stomach hurt and I had to throw up.

Then one day I overdosed on twelve Tylenol on the way to school. That was my inner realization. Right then my life flashed before my eyes.

After my suicide incident, I was forced to tell the rest of my family. My Grandmother Nancy worked in the hospital that I was in. She is a Jehovah's Witness. Of course, word got around, and everyone knew too soon that her grandson had been in the hospital. Luckily, she took the fact that I was gay well. But we will never have the same relationship that we used to, for her religion believes I am going nowhere good after death.

When you think of God, what do you feel? Do scriptures start popping up in your mind, or does your heart feel filled to overflowing with reverence and love? I should have always listened to my grandmother, Linda Sweet, when she warned me against organized religion. Religion evolves to the needs of our world. If I had stayed with the Jehovah's Witnesses, I would have deserted my family. Does that sound very godly to you?

I soon realized that in order to fully understand God, I must open my senses. I began to read spiritual inspiration books such as *Seat of the Soul* by Gary Zukav or *How to Know God* by Deepak Chopra.

It does not matter what the person is that you love, but who the person is. God is Love. It is the feeling you get when you gaze into the eyes of your lover. God did not make you this way or that, you did not make yourself this or that, you just are.

For me the whole image of God has changed from a vengeful, merciless deity to a loving, peaceful being that doesn't seek to convert, conform, or control. I now meditate daily to relieve stress, and I study other alternative medicines such as reiki and tai' chi. I no longer look at myself as a male or gay, I look at myself as a human, and if we all thought that way, the earth would be a much more peaceful place.

Being g/l/b/t is a long and tiring journey. Remember, we are normal just like everyone else. We are just a part of this ever-evolving earth. Whether or not people agree with it is their problem. I will always be myself without fear, knowing God is in my heart. I will stand up for my rights, respecting the rights of others, and fight until the day Humans are one and alike with Soul, regardless of personality.

That's not to say that religion wasn't a good experience for me. It has given me a foundation to build upon. It has given me the insight and wisdom I have today. To judge others is to unconsciously evaluate yourself. My mother always taught me to be open to things, and that is why I am the powerfully souled person I am today.

Everyday is a new day. Being g/l/b/t is a gift, not a fault. We are blessed, not cursed. We are brothers and sisters of the queer order and must stand up together to gain our lives. We are the future. We are here to open closed minds and test people for their kindness and compassion. Blessed be.

21

Elizabeth

"Are you and my mom lesbians?" It seemed safer to ask Rebecca, my mom's best friend and one of my favorite people. She was in the middle of divorcing her husband and had been living with us for about six months. I hadn't thought about their sharing a bed as anything other than chaste until someone on the bus had teased me about having a dyke for a mom. I brushed it off, but as the school year ended and I spent more and more time around my mom and Rebecca, I began to wonder if I wasn't being naive.

Rebecca, clearly uncomfortable, replied, "I'm going to have to talk to your mom before I answer that," which was clearly an answer in itself. I was reeling and in such shock that I don't remember the family conference my mom and Rebecca both swear took place with Rebecca's two kids, my older sister, and me. I don't recall my sister yelling at Rebecca, "I don't want you! I want a stepfather!" before running out of the room. Nor do I recall anything that we discussed. All I remember is feeling embarrassed at this development and planning to keep this "thing" secret as long as possible.

It was a secret that, for the most part, I was able to keep. For the most part because, unlike many other adolescents who find themselves different from the perceived norm, I had a safe place where I didn't have to hide my parent's identity. Camp Caz is a small United Church of Christ summer camp along the

Russian River in Northern California. It has been my spiritual home for as many years as I can remember. While I was growing up, it was the one place where I could be open about my home life. People there understood what it meant to have to pretend to be someone you weren't, because many of them had secrets they were afraid of revealing anywhere else too. I felt comfortable with people from camp because I didn't have to pretend to be someone else. I could just be me—the straight daughter of a lesbian—and that was fine. It was a community unlike anything else I'd experienced in life. At the time, I didn't realize that it was an incredible example of God and God's unconditional love made manifest in other people. It just felt safe. It was home.

There were other people who knew. Rebecca's two children were close to my age, and they obviously understood what I was going through. But they lived with their father, and it was hard to connect with them in that environment. Chrissy, a girl I met in junior high, had a mom who was a lesbian, too, and she sought me out to let me know that I could talk to her in confidence. I told only one other person in high school. As I looked out on 255 students on the day I spoke at my high school graduation, I could safely say that over 250 of them didn't know about my home life. This is not to say that people did not assume or suspect that my mom was a lesbian, but that was none of my concern.

I fled my hometown for New York City, a place where I hoped I could be open about my mother's sexuality. I didn't really hope that I could be open about it, I insisted on it. My introduction to strangers for four years was almost literally, "Hi, I'm Elizabeth and my mom's a lesbian." People who had a problem with it tended to stay away. I became an almost militant ally, a person who could be counted on to speak up for gays and lesbians, and someone that people could feel safe coming out to.

You may notice that God is almost absent from this story so far. This should not imply that God was absent from my life during this time. On the contrary, God was present in my life more strongly than you might expect. I attended Camp Caz faithfully throughout high school, experiencing unconditional love from my friends and counselors, and feeling safe for the only time in my adolescent life. Because of camp I never doubted God's presence or love for me, even when things were difficult at home. After graduating from high school, I began to counsel at Caz, where I began to pass on the love I had received to other teens.

For me, being a faithful Christian meant that I had a personal relationship with God. It did not mean that I had to go to church. In fact, the only times I went to church in high school or college were times when I visited a Catholic church with my then-boyfriend, and one Christmas eve service while in college. I certainly did not feel as though my experience of God would be accepted in congregations in my hometown. Even going to college in New York City, I felt bombarded by conservative messages that said that God, my "Father," hated and judged gays. Since this didn't speak to my life positively, I didn't feel the need to go. Camp remained my church in college.

The summer before I graduated from college, while counseling at Caz, my best friend Tom said to me, "You know, you should really be a youth minister." It was as if the world stopped. I had never actually considered doing what I did at Caz to be something I could do for a living. It was just what I did so that I could live with myself the other weeks of the year. Caz was my closest connection to a God whom I had always felt was near, but whom I'd never heard of supporting gay people. Since my only church experience for the last seven years had been Caz, I tried to brush off what Tom had said. Surely God wouldn't call a non-church-goer to ministry, would God? But I found Tom's words haunting me throughout my senior year of college. Though I studied Educational Theatre, I knew I didn't want to teach right after graduating. I began looking for jobs with some sense of purpose, which would allow me to explore other parts of myself that had been dormant for so long.

A few weeks after graduation, I felt a tug to find a church. I had been thinking about seminary more and more since graduation and I wanted some Christian fellowship nearby. To the surprise of my friends (many of whom didn't even know that Caz was a church camp), I picked a UCC church out of the phone book. Because it was a UCC church, I assumed it would be open to gays, lesbians, and their allies, but I was still nervous. Now I worried that people would judge me for not having gone to church for eight years. I worried about what my friends from college would think if they knew I was a Christian, much less a Christian considering parish ministry. In Broadway UCC, I found a tiny yet vibrant community with two women pastors. One was a married mom of two and the other was a lesbian in a committed relationship. I knew I had found my church home. My first Sunday, a couple sitting in front of me starting talking to me during the peace, and when they heard I was thinking about seminary, the husband gave me his business card. He was a minister at a different church that was hiring administrative assistants—was I looking for a job?

Could God be any more blunt with me? I have often laughed as I have recounted this story, because in retrospect my call is so obvious. Hello? Walk into church and find a job? A low-stress, nine-to-five job that pays all the bills and lets me figure out if parish ministry is my calling? Clearly God spoke to me that day, as surely as God spoke to me through my best friend. And at last I was ready to listen, to be faithful to my call.

I have become a member of Broadway UCC, formalizing the loving relationship I've felt with the church since that first Sunday, and with the denomination I've held so dear for so long. I work for that minister now. He is an associate pastor at Marble Collegiate Church, a large church that welcomes gays and lesbians. Since Broadway UCC has Sunday service in the afternoon, I'm also able to teach Sunday school at Marble in the morning. Working with the teens there, I felt that "Caz feeling" of loving and of being loved. After much prayer and patience, I realized that ordained youth ministry is my calling.

I will be going to Pacific School of Religion in Berkeley in the fall and I hope to be called to a vibrant parish like Broadway UCC someday. I hope to counterbalance the negative image portrayed by the Christian Right that so many people see with an image of a God who loves everyone, regardless of race, gender, class, or sexual orientation. I want to spread the "Caz feeling," which I now realize is God's love to others. After eleven years, my mom and Rebecca are far more open about their relationship. My hometown has changed and is far more gay-friendly than I perceived it was while I was growing up. I no longer feel as though I need to hide or explain away their living situation. I am proud of them, and of the way they struggled to raise me while closeted. I am honored God chose me to have two mothers, so that I can point to their life together as a symbol of God's transcendent love. Most of all, I am happy to finally be faithful to my calls: as the daughter of a lesbian, as a camp counselor, as a future ordained minister, as an ally of gays and lesbians, and, most importantly, as a Christian woman so grateful for God's grace and power to transform.

22

Charles

Those of you who know me know a few things about me: you know that I'm originally from Alabama, I'm a fan of southern literature, Mary Chapin Carpenter, and Vanderbilt football. You know I'm a social-justice-lovin', hymnal-totin', gonna-name-my-son-Wesley, diehard Methodist. I have the sticker on my car—you can go look. I'm proud to be part of the Methodist tradition—a tradition given to ending slavery, child labor, and debtors' prisons, a tradition where Scripture and reason and experience and tradition are valid ways of understanding Jesus. And you know I love the Wesley Foundation of the United Methodist Church.

But there's something you probably don't know about me that my family doesn't even know about me: I'm also gay. It's something that I have always felt, always known in my heart of hearts—which is not to say that I never struggled with it, that I never prayed to God to change me. I had heard enough TV preachers to understand that homosexuality was "wrong." In my teenage naivete, I read my Bible and all the concordance listings under "homosexuality."

I was devastated. How could the Bible, with all its talk about Jesus and love and justice and forgiveness, say these things about me? I thought there was only one solution: I had to change. Indeed, it was my desire to change that led me to the church in the first place. I was looking for a grace that I could name and manage, a grace that would do for me exactly what I demanded and would exact no inconvenience, offer no interference with the rest of my life. I was looking for a quick fix. Poof! With a stroke of God's hand, I'd be straight and my ticket would be punched for heaven. Amen, right?

Well, not exactly. That's not the kind of grace I found. By this time I was in college and I started to hear ministers talk about "the good gift of sexuality," "the theology of abundant grace versus the theology of scarcity," and "living the Jesus story," I found friends who talked about Jesus in a new and scary way, about how utterly human he was and how that was the point of his coming to earth, to make us aware of our full humanity. I read books that offered new ways of interpreting Scripture. And I prayed for guidance and grace.

And slowly it came. It was a subtle, quiet grace that taught me simply that Jesus loved me beyond anything else. Grace delivered a faith that said that we are to love our neighbors, to feed the hungry, clothe the naked, be with the poor. It has shaped my life in ways I can never express. Grace has defined me—not my sexual orientation.

23

Ben

My name is Ben. I am twenty-one years old, just graduated
from college, and have attended church all my life. My mother
is the organist at our church, so the Sunday morning trip was a
weekly childhood ritual. For me, going to church was much
more social than spiritual, more about coffee hour and friends
than God. I was active in church life—I served on a pastoral
search committee, and as president of the high school youth
group. But church was mostly something to do on Sunday
mornings, a tradition with little relevance to everyday life.

Middle school and high school were difficult, mostly due to
my growing feelings for other guys. Living in a rural community
and going to school at an athletic powerhouse made coming to
terms with my sexuality very difficult. This difficulty was ag-
gravated by the fundamentalist Christian Right's daily attacks
on the well-being of gay America. But even as hot a religious
topic as homosexuality was, I never heard any discussions
about gay, lesbian, bisexual, and transgendered people at my
home church. Recently I learned that there were many such discussions, but all between adults in closed-door committee meetings. I never got to take part in these discussions, or hear the
g/l/b/t supportive sermons preached while I was in Sunday
school. There were never hateful words in the air, but at the
same time I wasn't comfortable to be myself at church. I'll never
forget the time one well-meaning woman asked me if I was

going to bring my girlfriend to a potluck supper; I told her that I didn't have a girlfriend. What I burned to say was that she was asking the wrong questions, and that, no, I did not have a boyfriend. I felt invisible.

While in college I didn't attend church on a regular basis. My faith community was the summer camp I worked at, a camp run by the United Church of Christ. For four summers I lived on a lake and had a chance to see God's creation in action—I learned about the natural world, and came to appreciate the incredible beauty and power that is life. My experience with nature in this faith setting inspired me to think about God and religion, and while at camp I found a strong, personal connection with God. With this connection firmly established I had the opportunity to reconcile Christianity and gay sexuality.

I didn't know anyone at camp my first summer, but found out quickly that everyone knew I was gay. A friend of mine who had worked there the previous summer introduced me as her "gay friend Ben" to the camp staff. During my first week at camp, on a walk through the woods one day, a lifeguard told me that camp was a safe place to be gay. It turned out that I was working in a community with five other people who were gay, lesbian, or bisexual. This experience was the first time in my life that I didn't have to hide any part of my personality. The safe, loving community helped me grow and learn what it means to be a gay Christian. Many contemporary Christians think being a good Christian means winning souls for Jesus and keeping people from sinning against God. To me being a good Christian means spreading the love God has shared through Jesus. Jesus' message, the Good News, is that God loves all people and sacrificed Jesus to save us. In return we are expected to care for and love one another. God loves us all, including gay, lesbian, bisexual, or transgendered people.

Church camp is also where I met my first boyfriend. We had seen each other peripherally through high school, but camp staff was the first time we got to know each other. We built a friendship over the summer, a friendship largely based on our bond as the only two gay men at camp. I had a crush on him but never said anything about it. Then, on the last night of camp, he told me that he had feelings for me too—so we started dating. In our first year together our relationship faced many difficult challenges, but we stuck together and found ourselves back at camp the following summer.

Being a gay male couple working on staff at a Christian camp was a novel idea to me at the time—the stereotypical Christian summer camp isn't exactly open to gay couples. It turned out that the Christian part wasn't a problem, but rather the camp part. The daily switching from our professional relationship to our personal relationship was very difficult. We survived with a lot of support from the camp manager and our fellow staff members. The lessons about Christian love and the power of community I learned my first summer at camp were put into practice my second summer. We proved that a healthy, nurturing, gay relationship can be fostered by and grow in a Christian community. Being Christian and gay are not mutually exclusive; the two can work together to help us understand the world. In modern society g/l/b/t people are persecuted for who they are; early Christians were persecuted for what they believed. To our constant struggle for sexual equality we must bring lessons of love and reconciliation, not hatred, anger, and violence.

The one thing I want the world to know about g/l/b/t and questioning youth is that WE ARE HERE. Gay adults grow up from gay children, a fact both the straight establishment and the gay community should remember. Straight parents need to know that they are raising gay children—they need to understand the challenges that gay youth face. They need to provide us with safe homes, schools, churches, and neighborhoods. Gay adults need to remember their childhoods and help current g/l/b/t and questioning youth in any way they can. We need visible g/l/b/t role models, family, and friends. Adults both gay and straight need to support, not persecute, other adults who work with gay youth. We are young and we are gay, and we have been alone for too long.

24

Joe

All my life since I can remember I was made to go to a "born again" Christian church with my father and sister. I recently came out, in October of 1999, although I had known or had some intuition for about two to three years. I was brought up in a church where being gay/lesbian/bisexual/transgender was unheard of and immoral to even think about. I stopped going to church for about eight years of my life when my family up in New Hampshire was kicked out of the church in our hometown because my mother was a lesbian.

We started going to another church where we would attend every Sunday for two and a half years until my brother and sisters and I were harassed about our mother being a lesbian every Sunday in Sunday school. We left along with the pastor when she left for being lesbian and having too hard a time with some of the church members.

It was then that I felt as a young child that I never wanted to go to a church again. However, every time I visited my father I was made to go to church with him. The congregation there is so brainwashed by what they think the Bible says that they do not know the difference between the truth and the lies that come out of their own mouths. These people live in such a deluded fantasy that they don't know what the real world is like. They manipulate you and try to conform you into their ways of life. Since my father is a big part of that congregation and church, it was hard not to be "conformed."

My mother and sister and I attended five years at that church. I believe that the only way she was ever saved from turning into one of them was her upbringing. For twenty-one years my mother was taught to treat everybody equally and let them live for themselves and decide for themselves who they want to be. My mother was not about to throw all of that away and forget everything her parents taught her because the church had different views.

This, I believe was the only thing that saved me, too, from becoming a "born-again Christian." I am so thankful for that and the fact that I have now found an affirming church that welcomes and respects us for who we are that it brings great joy and happiness. Now that I have come out, it enlightens me to know that I can still go to a church like my Open and Affirming church and feel comfortable about myself and my peers. Church and Christ have become a huge part of my life now that I have come out. I have found faith and am well on the journey to find spirituality and eternal happiness in God.

25

Heather

The beginning of this coming-out story sounds like everyone else's, but how it ends is probably very different. I always had crushes on other girls. I thought that was completely normal. Only when I entered high school and it was still happening, that's when I got really scared.

My family is very religious. I was brought up in the Methodist church and am still a Methodist today. Everything I had ever heard about homosexuals was bad: "They're evil, they can change, they're going to hell," etc. So naturally I was terrified of my feelings and how people would react if they knew of them.

This terror turned me into such an adamant homophobe, it's hysterical! I remember my freshman year of high school in my English class, we had to write a letter to anyone of any importance. I wrote a letter to President Clinton telling him that gays should not be allowed in the military. I believe most of my reasoning for that was because gays would stare at other people in the shower and scare them. I wish I still had a copy of that letter!

Another thing this terror did for me—it sent me into a spiraling depression. I didn't want to go to hell. I didn't ask for these feelings. I knew people would hate me because nobody likes gays, especially not in my little town in Ohio. I was at my wit's end. I didn't know how to deal with my feelings, so I plunged myself into every school activity I could. I wanted to be (and was) so busy that I wouldn't have time to think about how lonely I was and about how much people would hate me if they knew. Above all, I was angry at God. What did I do to deserve such a punishment as being gay? I hated God for it. I prayed for God to make me straight again. With all this anger, hatred, despair, and loneliness building up inside me, it didn't take long for me to reach the suicidal stage.

Back at school, though, no one knew what I was going through. I had always been the one who kept everyone else's spirits up, so I hid my scared feelings from everyone. No one ever knew I was suicidal. I know this is how I developed my sense of humor. Making people laugh made everything seem okay. I didn't have to focus on my fear inside and it made them think nothing was wrong with me. Yet with every passing night at home, I came closer and closer to killing myself. I thank God that there was not a gun in my house. If we had had one I know I wouldn't be here today. But I had other ways of killing myself planned out. The most appealing one was by carbon monoxide poisoning in a car. The first person I came out to in high school was my best friend at the time. I thought if anyone would understand, she would. She seemed to be okay with it at first, but then she didn't speak to me for six months. That was the end of it, I thought. If she couldn't be okay with it then no one ever will be.

God is amazing. I know God exists because at those few moments when I came the closest to actually taking my own life, something told me not to. That something was God. I would be crying and convinced I would end it all that night, and then pictures of my family and friends would come into my head. "How would they react if you did this? They need you and you need them." Those are some of the thoughts that would go through my head. God kept me from killing myself by showing me what I had to live for. Yet above all, God loved me (and still does) for who I am. God was the one who told me to hang on. So I did. I wish I could describe that experience and feeling. Yet no words could do it justice. You have to feel it to really know. God is amazing.

I gave God a chance. I thought if God were telling me it would get better, then maybe it would someday. I made it through high school. College was like the mecca for me. I decided to start new and find friends who would love me for who I am.

College helped save me too. I came out the fall of my freshman year. I found queer groups and friends (gay and straight) who love me for who I am. I've made some of the best friends of my entire life here. Only I still had this huge obstacle right in front of me: my parents. What the heck was I going to tell them? Should I tell them? Would they kick me out?

I was growing tired of lying to them. They would ask me what I liked about college and how things were going. All I could answer with was "Oh, classes are great and I'm meeting lots of nice people." Inside, though, I was screaming "I'm gay and I'm having a great time! I'm good enough, smart enough, gay, and doggone it, people like me!" I can only imagine how they would've reacted if I had yelled that over the phone. I picture my poor parents passed out on the floor with the phone in their hands.

I knew my parents wouldn't kick me out. Their biggest question for me would be "What about your relationship with God?" I was still confused about religion and homosexuality too. Sure, God told me everything was cool, but I still got scared by the other Christians on campus who would assure me that gays are going to hell unless they change. Could I be wrong? I talked with a great campus pastor I had met. She's a lesbian and has helped guide me through my college years.

I came out to my pastor at my home church before I came out to my parents. Duane is a great guy. First off, when you can come out to your pastor and he's still there for you, it's an amazing thing! Duane admitted he didn't have all the answers, but he's helped me with my spiritual life so much. He told me he would help my parents after I told them too. Thank God for wonderful pastors!

I came out to my parents that first January of my freshman year. They took it pretty well and, as I had anticipated, their first question was "How is your relationship with God?" I told them it was fine. That was three years ago, and my parents are getting better every day, I think. I can tell they're still confused about what the Bible does say about homosexuality. I also know that they'd rather have me bringing home guys than women, but they're doing great. I told my brother right after I told them; he's pretty okay with it. He believes in the "love the sinner, hate the sin" thing, which is tough. I don't know how else to talk to him about it mainly because he doesn't like talking about it. But I'm working on that.

Where am I now? Happy to be a Christian. Obviously it's still quite a struggle to be out and safe. It's difficult being a queer Christian. Most churches don't like queers, and many queers don't like church. So many of us are right in the middle of it all. Yet I've decided that that is part of God's mission for me. I try to be the best bridge I can between the two communities. I wish I could convince all my queer friends that God does not hate them, but rather that He loves them and welcomes them. I've even gained the nickname "Rev" from all my queer friends here at school because I'm the most religious of the bunch.

Sexuality is a gift. God has taught me to embrace mine and to teach others that they should embrace theirs instead of fearing or hating it. I think we can take a good lesson from Yoda here: "Fear leads to anger. Anger leads to hate. Hate leads to suffering." It's incredible how this line can be applied to so many world situations.

I want everyone to know that it is possible to be a queer Christian. I want churches to know that they need to reach out to g/l/b/t youth. I don't want anyone to have to go through the pain and despair that I did. I try to speak to as many incoming college freshman classes as I can about being queer. G/l/b/t youth need to know that they're not alone and churches need to play a big role in that process.

I am still a Methodist today. As I watch the Methodist church flounder over the homosexuality issue and remove pastors from their congregations after they preside over gay marriages, all I can do is sigh. What is so wrong with the Methodist church that we cannot allow everyone to love each other? It makes me so angry sometimes.

Ordination is something I have thought much about in the past few years. I don't think I'll be able to do it for a while, but it crosses my mind fairly often. Yet who knows how long it would take for me to actually be allowed to be ordained in the Methodist church? To be turned away from your own denomination is a sad thing. I know not all Methodist churches turn away gays. There are many wonderful reconciling congregations out there. I hope they all know how important they are in this battle and how fabulous it is that they're actually reaching out and doing what God taught us to do: love.

I've only been out for a little over three years now, but as I look back on that incredible journey to coming out and then what has happened since I cannot help loving God even more. I have been through some incredibly difficult times. But you know, even though back then I was on the verge of suicide and have felt the full grip of helplessness, I would not go back and change one thing. That process made me who I am today: a strong, faithful, and loving queer Christian woman. I thank God for allowing me to live through and learn from such a powerful rite of passage. I have already reaped so many benefits from finding my strength in being queer and Christian.

I only wish that every young queer person could be able to make it like I did. But if churches keep pushing us out instead of stepping up and loving, how can we be surprised that one in three teenage suicides is because that young person was questioning her/his sexuality? Get out there and teach God's message of love. Jesus loves everyone. There are no clauses or footnotes in that statement saying "but only if you're straight." I am living proof that it is possible to be a queer Christian. My queerness is a gift from God and I thank God for it everyday.

Part Three

CHANGING
THE
LENS

26

A Guide for Parents[1]

The phone rings. I pick it up to hear a woman softly crying. Concern and relief fill her voice as she tells me about her fifteen-year-old son who had been missing for five days. They found him at the bus station in San Francisco. He told them he was gay, and that he just couldn't stand living in a small town and getting picked on at school anymore. She wants him to be safe, happy, and home.

An area teacher leaves a message for me that her daughter had just come out to her. "I don't think I'm homophobic, but I do feel a little shock. After all, I want grandchildren, and I don't want her life to be hard." She wants to come with her daughter and talk to me.

"Is this another phase she's going through? She's been changing friends, music, clothes, and religions about once a month lately. Now she tells us she's bisexual. What's this?"

"My son came out to us several months ago. I love and respect him. He's an eagle scout and I'm a scout leader. I don't know why, but for some reason I haven't gone back to scout meetings since this happened."

"I'm so worried about my son. After the workshop I could only think about my son. I really believe he's dealing with issues of gender identity. How do I help him? How can we talk about it?"

It was a beautiful Sunday afternoon, a rare event in New Hampshire spring seasons. I had been asked to speak at a

PFLAG (Parents and Friends of Lesbians and Gays) meeting. When I arrived I thought I must be late. Thirty adults were sitting in a circle, talking and listening intensely to one another. Except for the one person speaking, you could hear a pin drop. As I came through the door, several persons stood to greet me with broad and warm smiles, assuring me that I was not late. They have a support group meeting before the program, which is what I had walked in on. I glanced out the window towards the beautiful sunshine beckoning me. I wondered about these parents spending hours together. Are they desperate for companionship or committed to helping others? I quickly learned that the answer is both.

I related how I came out to my own parents when I was twenty-one, more than twenty years ago, and how my mother's response has unsettled me ever since. Upon hearing me say that I was a lesbian, she said about herself, "I'll never be able to sing in the church choir again." When I was twenty-one, that comment enraged me. Today I understand it better. A PFLAG father spoke up. "I get it. It's how I feel. I don't want to feel embarrassed or ashamed, or that my son's coming out is about me, but I do."

Family members are so deeply intertwined and connected with one another that often what one person experiences the others feel more deeply than they can explain or understand. This is especially true with parents and children. If one mixes in the cultural and theological meanings of sexual orientation and gender identity with this bond, combines it with the difficulties of raising a teenager, then adds whatever level of family function or dysfunction is present, it is no wonder that people become overwhelmed! If you are a parent and find yourself resonating at all with some of the previous statements, there may be some wisdom to be gleaned from the experiences of others. Remember, neither you nor your child is alone.

I tend to think of the journey of coming to terms with your child's sexual orientation or gender identity as a process of changing the lens, as on the body of a camera. You and your family have been viewing your child in a certain way for years. You've observed him or her through the lens of heterosexuality and/or traditional gender identity. All of your experiences, memories, visions, and hopes have been filtered through this particular viewpoint. For some of you, this has been a choice of values, but not for most. Most parents have simply taken on and assimilated the values of the culture, and our culture presumes that everyone is heterosexual and biologically gender identified until proven differently. Be aware, this is exactly what your child has gone through also. Perhaps since birth, your son or daughter has looked at him- or herself through the lens of presumed heterosexuality. Yes, he or she probably struggled with feeling different for a long time. But how was she or he to know that this feeling of difference meant nonheterosexuality or transgenderism until someone helped him or her figure it out? When the time comes, this lens is no longer viable. It just doesn't work. The image is fuzzy. If you want to see your child more clearly, go through the process with him or her. Take the old lens off, and put it in storage. Get the new lens, attach it to the body of the camera, and look more closely. If you take this step with your child, you will have work to do—emotionally, theologically, and socially—your world will change. It will be different, and it will probably be better. At least it will be real, and you will be able to keep your son or daughter in view.

No matter what your beliefs were about homosexuality and gender identity before your child came out to you, there is an initial step you must go through upon knowing what he or she has known for a while. You must grieve. In order to move beyond your assumptions of heterosexuality, you must first acknowledge them and let them go. You must let go of your dream that the most complicated issue of your child's prom night might be deciding what to wear. You must acknowledge that you were looking forward to a big church wedding—perhaps the kind your extended family expects. You must be aware of the many rites of passage and family process that are grounded in heterosexist and sexist assumptions. You must grieve that you have not known the deep struggle your child has worked through in order to get to the junction of telling you.

For many, coming out is a process that begins in grief. If we understand it that way, we can move more quickly into the new life it brings. In the book *Lesbian and Gay Youth: Care and Counseling,* the authors present a process by which parents and families adapt to a child's disclosure of lesbian or gay identity by working through each step in the grieving process. At first, parents are disbelieving, with questions and thoughts like, "Surely if this were true, I would have known." Or, "This can't be true. No one else in the family is gay. Everything has been so normal." Once a parent gets through this step, then he or she still must press against the reaction of denial. Several teens have told me that after coming out to their parents, the adults never mentioned it again. Often when people are feeling overwhelmed by something, they fall back on the mistaken notion that if we don't talk about it, it isn't true or will go away. This message of shame is not lost on your children. If you stay stuck here too long, don't expect him or her to talk openly with you again.

Upon moving through these two steps, parents must then face whatever guilt they may feel. The impact of social homophobia and heterosexism cannot be overstated here. No matter how liberal or progressive you may be, you are not exempt from the social beliefs and prejudices of our society. I have known liberal Unitarian Universalist parents horrified at their own level of shame and guilt upon their child's coming out, and have known conservative Baptists who surprised us all with their ease of acceptance. A lot of guilt may indicate other issues and dynamics that may need attention. For example, when my own mother exclaimed that she could no longer sing in the church choir, she was stating her assumption that her children were an extension of herself. Remember, your children are separate people, with identities and histories that intertwine with you but are not yours.

Once you move through whatever feelings of guilt or shame you carry, you may experience anger. Often, this comes out of parents' fears and concerns for their children and for themselves. There can be no doubt that life is harder for gay/lesbian/bisexual/transgender youth and adults than for their heterosexual peers. As parents become accustomed to the truth of their child's self-disclosure, they find that it is often not the sexual orientation itself that causes the most disturbance. Rather, it is the potential suffering their child must go through. Sometimes I watch helplessly as my own children are taunted with homophobic slurs because their mothers are lesbians. It breaks my heart to know that I cannot prevent this. The best any parent can do is model healthy coping, offer support, and advocate for your child when and where you can. Nonetheless, the anger still rises. Use the energy of anger to change the world. Don't take it out on your child.

Following the step of anger in the grieving process is that of sadness. Indeed, it is sad that you and your child have to go through any of this. Imagine the day when the stigma of homosexuality is removed, and children discover their sexual orientation as they discover their left-handedness, or their love of soccer or music. Sadness is normal. However, once again it is important not to stay immersed in sadness for too long, as it can turn into depression and emotional distancing from your child. Remember, children are in tune with their parents. Most children will intuitively pick up on a parent's sadness and interpret it as disappointment. Many youth have told me that they know their parents would prefer them to be straight. Be aware, your kids are watching, listening, and feeling for any and every response to their coming out.

Moving through grief is the process of removing the old lens from the camera body. The next step is replacing it with a new one, one that is accurate, sharper, and true. You have options of which lens to choose. You may select the lens of rejection, ambivalence, acceptance, or affirmation. If you reject your child's sexual orientation, you are rejecting your child. No one can separate from his or her sexuality. It is bred into our being—body and soul. You may believe that you can love your child and hate his or her sexual orientation (i.e., "Love the sinner, hate the sin"). You cannot. I have never known anyone—gay or straight, young or old—who felt that they were fully loved and cherished by people who rejected their sexual orientation. This lens exacts a heavy toll. For your child's sake and your own, please do not be naive about this.

Initially, the lens of ambivalence is the view that many parents take. You are not really sure about this new world your child is entering. You would really rather he or she risk and challenge less, but you will attempt to deal with what comes your way. Remember, the risks and challenges have been there all along. Now they are overt, and you have the chance to support and help your child. Never forget, the problem is not your son's or daughter's sexual orientation. The problem is homophobia.

Moving from ambivalence to acceptance is an important step. Acceptance means exactly that. You no longer give energy to longing for "the good old days," before parenting got even more complicated. You stop wondering if your child is going to come home and say, "April Fool's—only kidding . . . just wanted to see how you would react." You spend your energy parenting your gay, lesbian, bisexual, transgender, or questioning child. You sharpen the focus on the camera lens and see him or her as he or she is.

At some point you may find yourself joining those parents who affirm their children as sexual/spiritual young people, created in the image and likeness of God, not in spite of their sexual orientation, but along with it. At this point you can affirm that there is beauty and gift in your child's coming out. And so, you choose to come out too. You carry no shame. You advocate for your own son or daughter and for all gay/lesbian/bisexual/transgender youth and adults. I think of my many adoptive parents who year after year, meeting after meeting, phone call after phone call, march after march, legislative hearing after hearing, keep at it. I feel their love for me and my nonheterosexual brothers and sisters as they seek to make the world a better place for us all. I feel safer because of them. I thank God for them. Indeed, we are family.

As you walk this road, there are many questions you will have about yourself, your child, and your family. Don't expect your son or daughter to teach you everything. Do your own homework. When your children were toddlers, did you ask them when their bedtime should be, or how many sleepovers a week your eight-year-old should attend? Hopefully not. I imagine that you talked to other parents, read books, spoke with the pediatrician, and counted on some of your own childhood upbringing to inform you. Your teenager's or young adult's coming out is the same. You may have to search a little more for resources, but they are there. Talk to other parents. Speak with a professional you trust. Read affirming books. Work at understanding the messages about sexuality and sexual orientation that have been woven through the fabric of your family's life history. Essentially, you need what your child needs—accurate information, a community of support, and a willing spirit.

Finally, remember that you are still your child's parent, and your son or daughter is still your child. You need each other. Just because your child has gathered the strength and courage to come out doesn't mean that he or she doesn't need parents. The needs haven't changed as much as they have grown. Age-appropriate structure, household rules, and responsibilities need to remain in place along with openness, affirmation, unconditional love, and support. Yes, it is a new world, but some things remain the same.

Twenty-three years ago, when I came out to my parents, I had no idea how they might react then or in the future. I was twenty-one. Back then thirty seemed like old age! Your child may seem impatient with you now. He or she may long for you to get it faster than you are able. What teenager doesn't want that for their parents? Hang in with him or her. She/he needs you more than you can imagine.

"Love is patient . . . [and] kind. . . . [Love] does not insist on its own way; it is not irritable or resentful . . . [it] rejoices in the truth. [Love] bears all things, believes all things, hopes all things, endures all things" (1 Corinthians 13:4–7, NRSV).

27

Prayers and Worship

A PRAYER FOR YOUTH[1]

God of love . . .
we pray for the youth of our
    hearts
    homes
    churches
    society
    world.

We are quickly horrified
by the violent words and actions
of the public few
but not as often sickened
by the internal and external forces
that infect and distort their minds.

We pray for the parents of our youth.
Knowing full well that many of them
have their own struggles of mind and heart,
    by intervention of grace and
    community resources
may they be able to offer the
    love
    discipline
    example
that their youth so desperately need.

We pray for teachers and school administrators.
Knowing full well that they often work under
the most difficult and challenging conditions,
> by grace and
> community support
may they be able to offer the
> insight
> discipline
> example
> challenge
> support
that our youth so deserve.

We pray for our faith communities
that children and youth might be at
> the heart of our lives
> the focus of our prayers
> the recipients of our best resources
> and aware of our belief in them and our love for them.

God of love,
bless our youth . . .
and increase our concern and commitment
to their needs.
Amen.

PRAYER FOR COMING OUT AS GAY, LESBIAN, OR BISEXUAL

Creator God, I am learning things all the time. It is a gift to be young and to get to know you and your world, your beautiful creation.

I am also getting to know myself, and I'm discovering that sometimes I am attracted to members of my gender—other girls (or boys). Sometimes the things I feel are strong and deep. Sometimes it even feels like love. Sometimes I feel scared about these feelings. Sometimes I feel wonderful about them.

I know that I am your creation, and you have given me a wonderful gift in my orientation. I pray for your supporting presence as I become more comfortable with my feelings. I pray for your guidance, that I may know when it is the right time for me to let other people know about this part of me.

I pray for your supporting presence if I should be rejected, knowing that you, God who created me, will not reject me, that you will affirm me as part of your beautiful creation. In you I trust. Amen.

PRAYER FOR COMING OUT AS TRANSGENDER
(adaptation of preceding prayer)

Creator God, I am learning things all the time. It is a gift to be young and to get to know you and your world, your beautiful creation.

I am also getting to know myself, and I'm discovering that sometimes I feel as if I were the other gender. Sometimes I feel scared about these feelings. Sometimes I feel wonderful about them.

I know that I am your creation, and you have given me a wonderful gift in my gender identity. I pray for your supporting presence as I become more comfortable with my feelings. I pray for your guidance, that I may know when it is the right time for me to let other people know about this part of me.

I pray for your supporting presence if I should be rejected, knowing that you, God who created me, will not reject me, that you will affirm me as part of your beautiful creation. In you I trust. Amen.

CONGREGATIONAL PRAYER
Affirming Sexual and Genderal Minority Youth and Young Adults

Spirit of the Universe, Almighty One, this day we celebrate youth and young adults in our congregation. We celebrate the diverse gifts of a diverse people. We celebrate lesbians, gay men, bisexuals, and transgender young people among us, and welcome them as part of the body of God, as part of this unique assembly of your people.

We declare this a safe space for them, for we know there are places where young lesbians, young gay men, young bisexuals, and young transgender people do not feel safe or welcome.

We ask your special blessing on them, since we know you love them unconditionally. We ask you to empower us to love them— to love all—unconditionally in your great example. Amen.

PARENT'S PRAYER FOR A GAY, LESBIAN, BISEXUAL, OR TRANSGENDER SON OR DAUGHTER

God, you are the creator of the universe. You created all that is. You made the sun and the moon, the stars, and the seas. God who made the animals, and the fish and the birds, you created humanity. You created me, and you created the miracle that is my son (daughter), whom I love deeply.

I (we) have just learned that he (she) is gay (lesbian/bisexual/transgender). I (we) don't know why you created him (her) this way. Help me (us) not only to accept him (her) but to fully embrace and love him (her) for who he (she) is. I (we) ask for your presence during my (our) own journey with my (our) son (daughter).

I (we) also ask for your presence and special protection with my (our) son (daughter) on his (her) journey in this world, your world, which can sometimes be so cruel, especially to one who is different. I (we) ask your blessing on my (our) family. Amen.

A YOUNG PERSON'S PRAYER FOR GUIDANCE IN LOVE

Spirit, I feel butterflies in my stomach. Whenever I think about _____, I feel all tingly inside, and nervous, and excited. I ask for guidance from you, spirit of love, because I don't know if this is love or not. I don't know how she (he) feels, if it's mutual or not. Is it possible for _____ and me to be in love, two people of the same gender?

I think of Jonathan and David, and Ruth and Naomi, and wonder if they felt this same feeling, this same vulnerability and wonderfulness that I'm feeling. Did David feel tingly when he thought of Jonathan? Did Naomi feel nervous and unable to speak around Ruth? Did the centurion become giddy with delight thinking of his soldier? In the same way that they, too, may have prayed to you, I ask for your guidance, that I may know with certainty your love while you guide me to know if what I am feeling is in fact love.

I ask it for the highest good. Amen.

A PRAYER FOR GUIDANCE IN BECOMING SEXUALLY ACTIVE

Wonderful and loving God, I come to you now in this time and this space to ask for your guidance in deciding if I should have sex. You have given us this wonderful gift of sexuality to show our love and respect for another, to connect with another person deeply. You, loving Creator, gave this to us.

I ask for guidance now on my journey of deciding if now is the time for me to appreciate this gift more fully by using it. I bring to you my feelings for the other person. I bring to you, oh God, the enormity of this decision. I seek your guidance in knowing if this is the right time for me. Amen.

PRAYER FOR UNACCEPTING PARENTS/FAMILY

God, it feels painful right now. I hurt. I hurt because my parents (family) don't accept me for who I am, for who you made me to be. They're not happy that I'm a lesbian (gay/bisexual/transgender). Words of rejection have been said.

I ask you for two things. First, help me to understand that their own coming-out-as-parents (family) process may take a long time—it took me a long time, and it may take them a long time, too.

Second, I ask for your presence. Be with me as they begin a new journey. Be with them, too. Be with all of us. Right now we feel upset with each other and need to heal. Help us to love each other. Amen.

PRAYER FOR ACCEPTING PARENTS/FAMILY

Mountain-mover God, you have moved a mountain. I climbed the mountain of coming out to my parents (family), and I thank you because I am loved for who I am not only by you but also by them. It was risky—I could have been rejected—but I wasn't.

I give you thanks for that, and for them. Thank you for their love. Thank you for your love. They are both special gifts. Amen.

PRAYER FOR A FRIEND OR PEER WHO IS COMING OUT

Loving Spirit and Friend, my friend (_____) is coming out as transgender (lesbian/gay/bisexual). I ask for you to be present with my friend, to help her (him) know that she (he) is loved—by me, by you, and by others. Guide my friend as she (he) comes to terms with her (his) identity. Protect her (him) from the cruel things people may say and do; surround her (him) with support and with your love. Amen.

A DRAMATIC SCRIPTURAL LITANY
Based on Isaiah 55: 1–3; 12–13

"Leader" should be one person; readers 1, 2, 3, and 4 can be individuals or groups (e.g., "southwest side" or "balcony" or "choir"). Where there are choices, select only one to read but keep the others in mind (and/or in print).

LEADER: Lo, everyone who thirsts, come to the waters!
1: I'm thirsty!
2: Me too!
3: Yeah, me too!
4: I can't remember the last time I drank!
1, 2, 3: Let's drink!
4: But...
LEADER: and you that have no money, come, buy and eat!
1: Wow!
2: This is for us?
3: God must love us an awful lot.
4: I can't. I can't go.
LEADER: Come, buy wine and milk without money and without price.
4: I CAN'T!
1, 2, 3: What!!??

LEADER: Why do you spend your money for that which is not bread, and your labor for that which does not satisfy?

4: I said I can't! I can't drink! I can't eat!

1: But God said you can!

2: God said everyone who thirsts!

3: That means you too!

LEADER: Listen carefully to me, and eat what is good, and delight yourselves in rich food.

1: Let's go! Let's go drink!

2: Let's go eat!

3: It's free!

4: I can't! You don't understand. I'm not welcome. God doesn't want me.

LEADER: Incline your ear, and come to me; listen, so that you may live.

4: I'm listening! And I want to live! But they said I'm not welcome. They said I'm not welcome here, that you didn't mean me too.

1: What? What do you mean?

2: I don't understand.

3: We already said everyone's welcome.

4: But did you mean me? Sometimes everyone doesn't mean me.

LEADER: I will make with you an everlasting covenant, my steadfast, sure love for David.

4: You see, I'm a lesbian (a gay man, a bisexual, a transgender person). So does God really mean me? I've heard people say I'm not welcome. They say God doesn't want me, that I'm evil.

LEADER: Didn't you hear me? I will make with you an everlasting covenant.

4: Even with me? A lesbian (a gay man, a bisexual, a transgender person)?

LEADER: Are you thirsty? Are you hungry?

4: Yes. Yes, I'm thirsty. And hungry.

LEADER: Those are the only criteria.

4: Do you mean it?

LEADER: I will make with you an everlasting covenant.

4: This is amazing. God loves me, too!

1: Let's go!

2: Yeah, I'm thirsty too.

3: And I'm hungry!

4: Okay, I'm coming with you! We shall go out in joy.

LEADER: And be led back in peace.

1: The mountains and the hills before us shall burst into song.

2: And all the trees of the field shall clap their hands.

3: Instead of the thorn shall come up the cypress.

4: Instead of the brier shall come up the myrtle.

LEADER: And it shall be to the Lord for a memorial.

4: For an everlasting sign that shall not be cut off.

1, 2, 3, 4: That shall not be cut off!

ALL: You shall not be cut off!

BIBLICAL AFFIRMATIONS FOR TEENS AND ALL OF US![2]

1. "God honored us long ago by making us heirs without regard for our differences." (Galatians 3:28–29)

2. "You are called to freedom. Only do not use your freedom for self-indulgence. Live so that the gifts of the Spirit are visible in and through you." (Galatians 5:13, 16)

3. "I will praise you, God, for I am fearfully and wonderfully made. You have made me as I am; and I am your child." (Psalm 139:13–14)

4. "Practicing radical hospitality is perhaps one of the best ways that we heirs of God can give ourselves unreservedly in obedience to God." (Genesis 18–19)

5. "Jesus did not agree with the whole Levitical premise of exclusive holiness. It did not fit with his understanding of who God is or how God wants people to relate to each other." (Leviticus 18:22, Luke 10:25–37)

6. "Good News! God who has the power to accept or reject accepts and reconciles with all of us." (2 Corinthians 5:18)

7. "What is to be our response? As God's gentle heirs, we are to be new creations in Christ. We are to engage in reconciling ministries with each other." (2 Corinthians 5:18)

FINDING A SPIRITUAL HOME: PEER ROLE-PLAYS

1. Your roommate comes out to you as gay (lesbian). He (she) is afraid he (she) will go to hell for being a homosexual, and quotes Leviticus 18:22, "You shall not lie with a male as with a woman; it is an abomination." What do you say?

2. It is parent weekend. A friend has asked you to be present while she (he) tells her (his) parents she (he) is a lesbian (gay man).

3. Your campus minister tells you that she (he) has referred a young adult to an ex-gay change ministries and reparative therapy program. How do you react? What do you say to the campus minister?

4. A transgender young adult has begun to attend your campus ministry program. Some of the other students make rude comments. How do you react to the students? How do you interact with the transgender person?

5. Your campus faculty senate is considering a nondiscrimination policy. They have asked your campus ministry for advice. What things should the policy include? Sexual orientation? Gender identity? What is the role of your group as a recognized organization of people of faith on campus?

6. Parents of a friend call you over spring break because their son (daughter), your friend, has run away. He (she) has left a note making it clear that he (she) is struggling with his (her) sexual orientation and may be suicidal. You know where he (she) is, but fear for his (her) safety should he (she) return home.

7. You are bisexual. You are at a meeting of your campus ministry leadership council. You have participated in the group for three years and are an officer. The group wants to pass a resolution denying leadership positions to lesbian, gay, bisexual, or transgender people. Do you come out? Why or why not? What do you say?

8. You are a lesbian (gay man). You want to bring your girl-friend (boyfriend) to the campus ministry Christmas party. What do the two of you decide to do?

9. You are a transgender person. You feel called by God to ordained ministry. You discuss with your campus minister what may be facing you in your denomination and try to decide which seminary to attend next year.

10. You are attending an ecumenical gathering of college-age Christians away from home. You and a friend notice a peer you know attending the after-hours lesbian/gay/bisexual/transgender event, who sees you but pretends not to have noticed you. You did not before know this person's orientation/gender identity. Later, do the two of you offer support? Why or why not? If so, how?

28

Resources

BILL OF RIGHTS
For Lesbian, Gay, Bisexual, Transgender, and Questioning Youth and Young Adults in the United Church of Christ

Written by Timothy Brown with special thanks to Virginia Uribe and Project 10

The right to fair and accurate information about sexual orientation and gender identity in Sunday school materials, youth group materials, church publications, and textbooks.

The right to unbiased information about the historical and continuing contributions of lesbians, gays, bisexuals, and transgender people in the United Church of Christ, in Christianity, and in other religions.

The right to positive role models, both clergy and laity, both in person and in the curriculum; the right to accurate and nonjudgmental information about themselves that is delivered by training people who both inform and affirm lesbian, gay, bisexual, transgender, and questioning youth and young adults.

The right to attend all churches and events free from verbal and physical harassment, where religious practice, not survival, is the priority.

The right to attend churches where respect and dignity for all youth and young adults, including lesbian, gay, bisexual, transgender, and questioning youth and young adults, is a standard set by the United Church of Christ, supported by respective national, conference, and association youth and young adult ministries groups, and enforced by every national, conference, and association staff, lay worker, and clergy member.

The right to be included in all support programs that exist to help youth and young adults deal with the difficulties of adolescence.

The right to be included in all social and other support programs specifically for lesbian, gay, bisexual, transgender, and questioning youth and young adults.

The right to association, conference, and General Synod delegates who advocate for their freedoms, rather than association, conference, and General Synod delegates who reinforce hatred and prejudice.

The right to a heritage free of crippling self-hate and unchallenged discrimination.

The right to the sustaining and nurturing love of God.

UNITED CHURCH OF CHRIST GENERAL SYNOD RESOLUTION:
Prevention of Lesbian, Gay, Bisexual, and Transgender Youth Suicide

As adopted by General Synod XXII, UCC, Providence, RI, 1–6 July 1999

WHEREAS, the General Synod of the United Church of Christ has declared itself supportive of youth in the United Church of Christ;

WHEREAS, the General Synod of the United Church of Christ has called upon settings of the church to declare themselves Open and Affirming of gay and lesbian persons; and

WHEREAS, ignorance of, and silence about, youth suicide in general and in particular of gay, lesbian, bisexual, transgender, and questioning youth is present in the United Church of Christ and churches of all denominations and in society in general;

THEREFORE, BE IT RESOLVED that we, the delegates to the Twenty-second General Synod of the United Church of Christ, meeting in Providence, Rhode Island, July 1–6, 1999, pledge to take actions that will increase awareness of and seriously address youth suicide and the link between youth suicide and sexual or gender identity, by encouraging open discussion of these issues in our families, churches, youth groups, associations, conferences and camps;

BE IT FURTHER RESOLVED that the United Church Board for Homeland Ministries (or its successor body) be requested to conduct a research study analyzing the role of religion in lesbian, gay, bisexual, and transgender youth suicides and develop resources and educational materials concerning these issues and distribute them for use by local churches, associations, conferences and other settings of the United Church of Christ;

BE IT FURTHER RESOLVED that the ministries and various settings of the United Church of Christ be strongly encouraged to identify and use, as soon as possible, existing educational materials directed to youth, clergy, parents, and laity, which will assist them in understanding:
1) youth suicide;
2) sexual orientation and gender identity; and,
3) how the above two issues relate;

BE IT FURTHER RESOLVED that the ministries of the United Church of Christ in all its settings raise these issues ecumenically, particularly with, but not limited to, our partner churches, The Christian Church (Disciples of Christ), The Presbyterian Church (USA), The Evangelical Lutheran Church in America, and The Reformed Church in America, in local interfaith networks; and

BE IT FURTHER RESOLVED that the United Church of Christ, in all its settings, reflect on what leads youth to a loss of hope and faith.

BE IT FURTHER RESOLVED that the ministries and various settings of the United Church of Christ work to make the existence of open and affirming churches known to lesbian, gay, bisexual, transgender, and questioning youths;

BE IT FINALLY RESOLVED that the United Church of Christ in all its settings raise these issues with civil authorities, in their community and legislative settings, and with schools and families; and that the Office for Church in Society (or its successor body) facilitate these efforts and advocate in a similar fashion, to ensure that issues of lesbian, gay, bisexual, transgender, and questioning youth suicide are adequately addressed in society at large.

Funding for this action will be made in accordance with the overall mandates of the affected agencies and the funds available.

This resolution was presented to the 1999 General Synod of the United Church of Christ by the Hudson Mohawk Association of the New York Conference; the Metropolitan Denver Association of the Rocky Mountain Conference; Community UCC, Boulder, Colorado; First Congregational UCC, Boulder, Colorado; and the Montana-Northern Wyoming Conference. It was also endorsed by the coordinating committee of the Association of United Church Educators. The General Synod, which met in Providence, overwhelmingly approved the resolution entitled Prevention of Lesbian, Gay, Bisexual, Transgender, and Questioning Youth Suicide.

UNITED CHURCH OF CHRIST GENERAL SYNOD RESOLUTION CALLING ON UNITED CHURCH OF CHRIST CONGREGATIONS TO DECLARE THEMSELVES OPEN AND AFFIRMING

Adopted by General Synod XV, UCC, Ames, IA, 2 July 1985

WHEREAS, the Apostle Paul said that, as Christians, we are many members, but we are one body in Christ (Romans 12:4), and Jesus calls us to love our neighbors as ourselves (Mark 12:31) without being judgmental (Matthew 7:1–2) nor disparaging of others (Luke 18:9–14); and

WHEREAS, recognizing that many persons of lesbian, gay, and bisexual orientation are already members of the church through baptism and confirmation and that these people have talents and gifts to offer the United Church of Christ, and that the UCC has historically affirmed a rich diversity in its theological and biblical perspectives; and

WHEREAS, the Tenth through Fourteenth General Synods have adopted resolutions encouraging the inclusion, and affirming the human rights, of lesbian, gay, and bisexual people within the UCC; and

WHEREAS, the Executive Council of the United Church of Christ adopted in 1980 "a program of Equal Employment Opportunity which does not discriminate against any employee or applicant because of . . . sexual orientation"; and

WHEREAS, many parts of the church have remained conspicuously silent despite the continuing injustice of institutionalized discrimination, instances of senseless violence, and setbacks in civil rights protection by the Supreme Court; and

WHEREAS, the church has often perpetuated discriminatory practices and has been unwilling to affirm the full humanness of clergy, laity, and staff with lesbian, gay, and bisexual orientation, who experience isolation, ostracism, and fear of (or actual) loss of employment; and

WHEREAS, we are called by Christ's example to proclaim release to the captives and set at liberty the oppressed (Luke 4:18); and

WHEREAS, examples of covenant of Openness and Affirmation and Nondiscrimination Policy may be found in the following:

EXAMPLE 1: COVENANT OF OPENNESS AND AFFIRMATION

We know, with Paul, that as Christians, we are many members, but are one body in Christ—members of one another, and that we all have different gifts. With Jesus, we affirm that we are called to love our neighbors as ourselves, that we are called to act as agents of reconciliation and wholeness within the world and within the church itself.

We know that lesbian, gay, and bisexual people are often scorned by the church, and devalued and discriminated against both in the church and in society. We commit ourselves to caring and concern for lesbian, gay, and bisexual sisters and brothers by affirming that:

> *we believe that lesbian, gay, and bisexual people share with all others the worth that comes from being unique individuals;*
> *we welcome gay, lesbian, and bisexual people to join our congregation in the same spirit and manner used in the acceptance of any new members;*
> *we recognize the presence of ignorance, fear, and hatred in the church and in our culture, and covenant to not discriminate on the basis of sexual orientation, nor any other irrelevant factor, and we seek to include and support those who, because of this fear and prejudice, find themselves in exile from a spiritual community;*
> *we seek to address the needs and advocate the concerns of lesbian, gay, and bisexual people in our church and in society by actively encouraging church instrumen-*

*talities and secular governmental bodies to adopt and
implement policies of nondiscrimination; and*
*we join together as a covenantal community, to celebrate
and share our common communion and the reassur-
ance that we are indeed created by God, reconciled by
Christ, and empowered by the grace of the Holy Spirit.*

EXAMPLE 2: INCLUSIVE NONDISCRIMINATION POLICY
We do not discriminate against any person, group, or organization in hiring, promotion, membership, appointment, use of
facility, provision of services, or funding on the basis of race,
gender, age, sexual orientation, faith, nationality, ethnicity,
marital status, or physical disability.

THEREFORE, the Fifteenth General Synod of the United Church
of Christ encourages a policy of nondiscrimination in employment, volunteer service, and membership policies with regard to
sexual orientation; encourages associations, Conferences, and all
related organizations to adopt a similar policy; and encourages
the congregations of the United Church of Christ to adopt a nondiscrimination policy and a Covenant of Openness and Affirmation of persons of lesbian, gay, and bisexual orientation within
the community of faith.

Notes

Preface

1. The Welcoming Church movement is an ecumenical program of study through which churches declare themselves to be fully supportive and inclusive of gay, lesbian, bisexual, and transgender persons in all aspects of church life and leadership. Contact your denomination for more information.

Chapter 1

1. A. R. D'Augelli and S. L. Hershberger, "Lesbian, Gay, and Bisexual Youth in Community Settings: Personal Challenges and Mental Health Problems." *American Journal of Community Psychology* 21: 421, 1993.

2. G. M. Herek, "Documenting Prejudice and Violence Against Lesbians and Gay Men: The Yale Sexual Orientation Study." *Journal of Homosexuality* 25: 18, 1993.

3. Homophobia is a form and manifestation of prejudice, or prejudgement. It is a combination of beliefs, attitudes, and opinions that one has pre-formed, based on myths, assumptions, and stereotypes.

4. R. R. Troidan, "The Formation of Homosexual Identities," *Journal of Homosexuality,* 17: 43, 1989.

5. Ryan Caitlin and Donna Futterman, *Lesbian and Gay Youth: Care and Counseling.* (New York: Columbia University Press, 1998), 11.

Chapter 2

1. Christian de la Huerta, *Coming Out Spiritually: The Next Step* (New York: Putnam Books, 1999), forward.

2. John H. Westerhoff, *Will Our Children Have Faith?* (New York: The Seabury Press, 1976), 89.

3. Westerhoff, 92.

4. de la Huerta, 169.

Chapter 26

1. Leanne Tigert, adapted from a presentation at PFLAG (Parents and Friends of Lesbians and Gays) New Hampshire, March 2000.

Chapter 27

1. By the Reverend Dick Sparrow, Central Area Conference Minister, Massachusetts Conference, UCC.

2. Mary Jo Osterman, *Claiming the Promise: An Ecumenical Bible Study Resource on Homosexuality* (Chicago: Reconciling Congregation Program, 1997), 12, 13, 19, 32, 38, 41. The quotes are reflections on the biblical passages cited. As cited in *Open Hands* 13, no. 1 (Summer 1997).

Bibliography

For Young People

Alyson, Sasha, ed. *Young, Gay, and Proud.* Boston: Alyson Publications, 1991.

Bass, Ellen, and Kate Kaufman. *Free Your Mind: The Book for Gay, Lesbian, and Bisexual Youth and Their Allies.* New York: Harper Collins, 1996.

Bauler, Marion Dane, ed. *Am I Blue? Coming Out from the Silence.* New York: Harper Collins, 1993.

Brinner, Larry. *Being Different: Lambda Youth Speak Out.* Guilford: Franklin Watts, 1996.

Chandler, Kurt. *Passages of Pride: True Stories of Lesbian and Gay Teenagers.* Boston: Alyson Publications, 1997.

Chandler, Kurt, and Mitchell Ivers. *Passages of Pride: Lesbian and Gay Youth Come of Age.* New York: Times Books, 1995.

Due, Linnea A. *Joining the Tribe: Growing Up Gay and Lesbian in the '90s.* New York: Anchor Books, 1995.

Grima, Toni. *Not the Only One: Lesbian and Gay Fiction for Teens.* Boston: Alyson Publications, 1995.

Heron, Ann, ed. *Two Teenagers in Twenty: Writings by Lesbian and Gay Youth.* Boston: Alyson Publications, 1994.

Mastoon, Adam. *The Shared Heart: Portraits and Stories Celebrating Lesbian, Gay, and Bisexual Young People.* New York: Lathrop, Lee and Shepard, 1997.

Savin-Williams, Ritch C. *And Then I Became Gay: Young Men's Stories.* New York: Rutledge, 1997.

Scholinski, Daphne, and Jane Meredith Adams. *The Last Time I Wore a Dress.* New York: Putnam Publishing Group. 1997.

Sherill, Jan-Mitchell, and Craig Hardesty. *Gay, Lesbian, and Bisexual Students Guide to Colleges, Universities, and Graduate Schools.* New York: NYU Press, 1994.

Singer, Brett. *Growing Up Gay/Growing Up Lesbian: An Anthology for Young People.* New York: New Press, 1993.

Stewart, Gail B., and Natasha Frost. *Gay and Lesbian Youth.* San Diego: Lucent Books, 1997.

Jennings, Kevin. *Becoming Visible: A Reading in Gay and Lesbian History for High School and College Students.* Boston: Alyson Publications, 1994.

Lesbian/Gay/Bisexual/Transgender Studies

Blumenfeld, Warren J., ed. *Homophobia: How We All Pay the Price.* Boston: Beacon Press, 1992.

Brown, Mildred, and Chloe Ann Rounsley. *True Selves: Understanding Transsexualism for Families, Friends, Coworkers, and Helping Professionals.* San Francisco: Jossey-Bass Publishers, 1996.

Comstock, Gary David. *Unrepentant, Self-Affirming, Practicing: Lesbian/Bisexual/Gay People Within Organized Religion.* New York: Continuum Publishing Group, 1996.

Helminiak, Daniel. *What the Bible Really Says About Homosexuality.* San Francisco: Alamo Square Press, 1994.

Hutchins, Lorraine, and Lani Kaahumanu. *Bi Any Other Name: Bisexual People Speak Out.* Boston: Alyson Publications, 1991.

Kissen, Rita. *The Last Closet: The Real Lives of Lesbian and Gay Teachers.* Portsmouth, NH: Heinemann, 1995.

Perez, Ruperto, Kurt A. DeBord, and Kathleen J. Bieschke, eds. *Handbook of Counseling and Psychotherapy with Gay, Lesbian, and Bisexual Clients.* Washington: American Psychological Association, 2000.

Pharr, Suzanne. *Homophobia: A Weapon of Sexism.* Little Rock: The Women's Project: Chardon Press, 1988.

Ramsey, Gerald. *Transsexuals: Candid Answers to Private Questions.* Freedom, CA: Crossing Press, 1996.

Roscoe, Will, and Gay American Indians. *Living the Spirit: A Gay American Indian Anthology.* New York: Saint Martin's Press, 1988.

Tigert, Leanne McCall. *Coming Out Through Fire: Surviving the Trauma of Homophobia.* Cleveland: United Church Press, 1999.

Tigert, Leanne McCall. *Coming Out While Staying In: Struggles and Celebrations of Lesbians, Gays, and Bisexuals in the Church.* Cleveland: United Church Press, 1996.

Griffen, Carolyn Welch, Marian J. Wirth, and Arthur G. Wirth, eds. *Beyond Acceptance: Parents of Lesbians and Gays Talk About Their Experiences.* New York: St. Martin's Griffen Press, 1996.

Lesbian/Gay/Bisexual/Transgender Youth Studies

Decrescenzo, Theresa. *Helping Gay and Lesbian Youth: New Policies, New Programs, New Practice.* Binghamton: Haworth Press, 1994.

Harris, Mary B. *School Experiences of Gay and Lesbian Youth: The Invisible Minority.* Binghamton: Haworth Press, 1998.

Herdt, Gilbert, and Andrew Boxer. *Children of Horizons: How Gay and Lesbian Teens Are Leading a New Way Out of the Closet.* Boston: Beacon Press, 1993.

Herdt, Gilbert, ed. *Gay and Lesbian Youth.* New York: Harrington Park Press, 1989.

Owens, Robert. *Queer Kids: The Challenges and Promise for Lesbian, Gay, and Bisexual Youth.* Binghamton: Haworth Press, 1998.

Ramafedi, Gary, M.D., M.P.H., ed. *Death by Denial: Studies of Suicides in Gay and Lesbian Teenagers.* Boston: Alyson Publications, 1994.

Ryan, Caitlin, and Donna Fetterman. *Lesbian and Gay Youth: Care and Counseling.* New York: Columbia University Press, 1998.

Whitlock, Katherine. *Bridges of Respect: Creating Support for Lesbian and Gay Youth.* Philadelphia: American Friends Service Committee, 1988.

Contributors

LEANNE, European-American, Concord, New Hampshire,
United Church of Christ

TIMOTHY, European-American, Greeley, Colorado,
United Church of Christ

ANNE, age 17, European-American, Deerfield, New Hampshire,
United Church of Christ

AMANDA, age 21, European-American, Contoocook, New Hampshire,
United Methodist

RYAN, age 17, Latino, California, United Methodist

SHAWN, age 21, European-American, Glendale, Arizona,
Presbyterian Church (USA)

AMY, age 19, European-American, Portland, Maine,
Unitarian Universalist Association

TOLONDA, age 22, African-American, Connecticut,
United Church of Christ

KENNETH, age 17, Mexican-American, Arizona, Wiccan

JANÉE, age 21, European-American, Grand Rapids, Michigan,
Conservative Baptist

TESIA, age 21, European-American, Fairfax, California,
United Church of Christ

ERIC, age 24, European-American, Boston, Massachusetts,
Reformed Jewish

CHAD, age 20, European-American, Key West, Florida,
Episcopal Church

JEFFREY, age 20, European-American, Boston, Massachuetts,
United Methodist

HEATHER, age 21, European-American, Concord, New Hampshire,
Catholic

MATTHEW, age 20, European-American, Philadelphia, Pennsylvania, United Church of Christ

BOBBI, age 22, European-American, Ohio, United Methodist

NATHAN, age 14, European-American, Belmont, New Hampshire, Wiccan

ELIZABETH, age 23, European-American, Berkeley, California, daughter of a lesbian, United Church of Christ

CHARLES, age 21, European-American, Nashville, Tennessee, United Methodist

BEN, age 21, European-American, Bangor, Maine, United Church of Christ

JOE, age 17, European-American, New Hampshire, Interdenominational

HEATHER, age 21, European-American, Dayton, Ohio, United Methodist

Other books from The Pilgrim Press

COMING OUT THROUGH FIRE
Surviving the Trauma of Homophobia

Leanne McCall Tigert

0-8298-1293-8/144 pages/paper/$12.95

Tigert presents an inside look at the trauma of being lesbian, gay, or bisexual in a heterosexual world. Discussing the trials that these persons endure everyday, she examines the church, the effects of HIV and AIDS, and family issues—and provides hope by offering a "new life" that will allow recovery from the trauma inflicted by church and society. Study questions for reflection and discussion are included.

COMING OUT WHILE STAYING IN
Struggles and Celebrations of Lesbians, Gays, and Bisexuals in the Church

Leanne McCall Tigert

0-8298-1150-8/208 pages/paper/$14.95

Tigert shares stories of those in the church who are lesbian, gay, or bisexual. She shares the history of justice for those people in various denominations, along with the stories and reflections of individuals with psychological and theological interpretations. Tigert develops a fresh theology of liberation and suggests ministries to empower this audience. Study questions are included to stimulate individual reflection and group discussion.

COMING OUT TO PARENTS
A Two-Way Survival Guide for Lesbians
and Gay Men and Their Parents
Revised and Updated

Mary V. Borhek

0-8298-0957-0/320 pages/paper/$15.95

Revised and updated, this best-selling classic examines coming out in the age of AIDS as well as the latest religious views.

MY SON ERIC

Mary V. Borhek

0-8298-0729-2/168 pages/paper/$11.95

A classic account of a mother's struggle to understand and accept her gay son—from denial to reconciliation to activism. A touching and courageous true story, particularly useful for those parents whose religious backgrounds condemn homosexuality.

NOW THAT YOU'RE OUT OF THE CLOSET,
WHAT ABOUT THE REST OF THE HOUSE?

Linda Handel

0-8298-1244-X/244 pages/cloth/$20.95

A witty and helpful book that provides solid advice for gays and lesbians. It covers a full range of life concerns—including lingering childhood issues, dating, sex and love, intolerance, and self-hatred—in a way that is direct, open, and honest. Each chapter concentrates on a specific issue such as self-worth, dating, abusive relationships, and developing a gay spirituality.

To order call The Pilgrim Press
1-800-537-3394